BOXFORD THROUGH THE AGES

BOXFORD
THROUGH THE AGES

A NEW HISTORY

ROGER LOOSE
M.A. (Cantab.)

ORPHEAN PRESS
2021

First published in 2021 by Orphean Press
10 Heath Close, Polstead Heath, Colchester CO6 5BE
Second impression 2021

ORPHEAN

PRESS

Typeset in 9 on 12-point Typotheque William Text,
printed and bound in Great Britain by Peter Newble:
10 Heath Close, Polstead Heath, Colchester CO6 5BE
peter@newble.com · http://www.newble.com/

2021

ISBN 978-1-908198-21-1

British Library Cataloguing in Publication Data
A catalogue record for this book is
available from the British Library.

For those who know and love this unique place

The historic heart of Boxford, viewed from the south in 2018.

CONTENTS

CONTENTS

The south porch of St Mary's church, started in 1441 following bequests, was built with Caen limestone, originating in Normandy and brought on flat-bottomed boats up the River Box.

LIST OF ILLUSTRATIONS

ACKNOWLEDGEMENTS

My grateful thanks are due to: my wife, Tina, for her constant encouragement and support in researching this material, proof reading and bringing it to fruition; Boxford Society members, past and present, who have unknowingly provided the stimulus over the last twenty-seven years to find the material on which I have drawn; and Peter Newble, who, with his great knowledge and love of Boxford and through his expertise in editing and publishing, added immeasurably to this book.

Church Street as Norman Scarfe saw it in 1960 with 'nicely re-fronted' houses from the sixteenth and seventeenth centuries. The bypass was not built for another fifteen years and yet there is not a car in sight.

INTRODUCTION

'HISTORY is that certainty produced where the imperfections of memory meet the inadequacies of documentation.'

JULIAN BARNES, 2011

THIS is very true of the account that follows. Boxford unfortunately lacks documentary evidence for much of its history. There are no manorial court records or rolls from the Middle Ages, for example, as there are for some similar Suffolk parishes. The following story therefore sometimes draws on detail recorded in those parishes to re-construct life here in Boxford. It is not always 'certainty', but it is well-founded and intended to provide real insight into the lives of those who came before us in this lovely village.

I have often been asked after my village history talks to 'write it down'. This is my attempt and it draws heavily on the archive held by the Boxford Society and the writings of several past members, sadly no longer with us. Sources are not listed because I have drawn from such a huge variety, ranging from the well-researched tomes of historians through to scribbled, handwritten notes and memories. This is my own individual, descriptive history with some interpretation. It is not an academic study. You should know that I have been careful to draw upon only those sources I thought I could trust. I am most grateful to my wife, Tina Loose, for her wide knowledge of the archive and for patiently running up and downstairs searching out records on demand. All history is selective in what it includes and what it leaves out, and this is no exception. Please tell me if you have evidence that suggests that I have got my facts wrong.

In 1960 in the *Shell Guide to Suffolk*, Norman Scarfe, the author and famous Suffolk landscape historian, noted that Boxford 'is a village of charm, nestling in valley bottom; perfect village'. He was referring to the way it then looked, hidden snugly in its valley and clustered around its late-Mediaeval church alongside the River Box. He was seeing streets of mainly fifteenth-century to seventeenth-century, timber-framed, terraced houses, albeit often 'nicely refronted'. No-one living here today would surely argue with his description, even though the 'perfect village' is much expanded since his day and is to-day being threatened by a mass of new suburban-style housing and far too many cars. We should remember that Scarfe was writing be-fore much modern housing was built and before mass car ownership dominated the centre of the village and replaced walking.

The following history seeks to describe and explain the evolution of Boxford and its people over the last 1,500 years. The reasons for the location and very early development of the settlement is deduced from the geography and archaeology of the surrounding landscape, since written records only began about 900 years ago. From then on its growth is increasingly recorded and provides the evidence and oral memory that allows us to discover what it was like living here for our predecessors.

This fifty-five million-year-old 'sarsen' stone is a very hard, fine sandstone. There are at least 160 more sarsens lying on the surface elsewhere in the parish.

I
EARLY ORIGINS

THE solid bedrock underlying Boxford is London clay, which actually includes silt and sand. It lies thinly on upper chalk, the surface of which here is buried at 15m above present sea level. Surprisingly, therefore, the chalk stratum lies only 10m beneath your feet at Boxford Post Office. Before the Ice Ages these rocks would have formed the land surface. The landscape would have been much more undulating, being cut more deeply by streams and rivers. Over one hundred and sixty 'sarsen' stones have been found at or close to the surface within the parish. These fifty-five-million-year-old rocks are very hard, fine sandstone blocks weathered from within the London clay. They are today found scattered on or near the surface, or have been moved to useful places. They often protect the corners of buildings. There is a splendid 'mammillated' sarsen, illustrated opposite, at the foot of the Croft on Broad Street. Originally one was placed at each end of the bridge or ford, but only that on the southern side now remains.

When the 1km-deep ice sheet of the Anglian glaciation passed over and completely covered Boxford about 450,000 years ago, it ground down the land surface. As it melted it left a thick mask of clay, gravels and sand over the landscape, smoothing it out. Before the ice sheet the Box river and streams had carved out a very deep valley in the chalk as it flowed to an Ice-Age sea surface which was about 60m below its present level. This valley was then filled with sands and gravels. Where the valley is wider it was later further filled with river deposits of alluvium supporting fen, marshland and meadowland. The surrounding gravelly and sandy slopes today rise quite rapidly from this valley floor to a flat or gently rolling plateau, mainly covered by

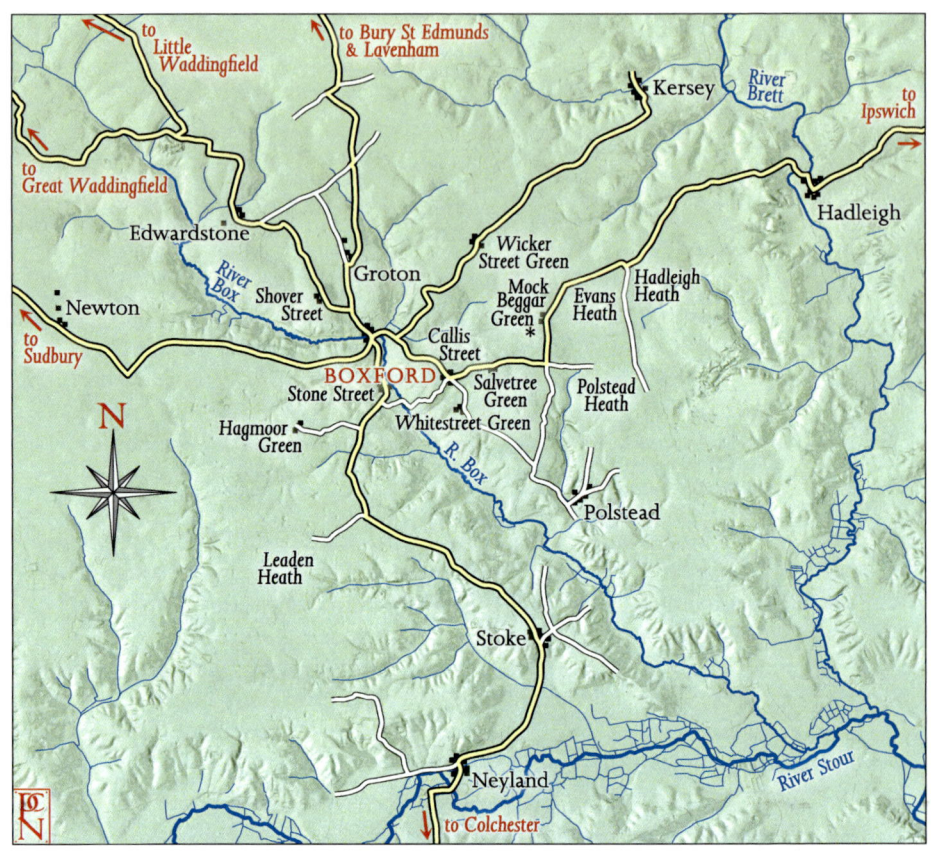

ANCIENT TRACKWAYS

CONVERGING ON THE FORD AT BOXFORD

Placenames as recorded in 1799 by Charles Verron for the Ordnance Survey

* Mock Beggar Green now known as Bower House Tye

SCALE 1:108,675
1 inch : 1¾ miles approximately

0   1   2   3 miles

0 1 2 3 4 5 km

Main tracks	
Minor tracks	
Rivers	
Streams	
Ancient trackway settlements	⟍

chalky boulder clay, at about 40–50 m above present sea level on either side.

The earliest traces of human activity are mainly 'accidental' losses such as the Middle Bronze Age bronze quoit-headed pin from around 1200 BC found in 1980 in the bed of the Groton brook, by the bridge at the junction of Broad Street and Ash Street. An earlier hand axe and flint tools have also been found. These people would have been mainly animal rearers on the drier valley sides. During the Iron Age, despite the invention of the iron plough, few inroads were made onto the heavier soils of the plateau above.

The first evidence of permanent settlement here was the discovery of a Belgic cremation cemetery for six people with associated pots, jewellery and domestic goods at Whitestreet Green, which was in the parish of Boxford until 1974. It is thought that this area was only sparsely populated before the arrival of Belgic migrants around 10 BC to AD I. These new arrivals seem to have integrated with the local Trinovantes tribe that ruled this area from Camulodunum (Colchester) before it became Roman territory in AD 43, when the local tribes were subdued.

Finds of Roman coins and broken pottery are numerous, but the most notable find was the seated bronze figurine of the deity Mercury found close to the old Hadleigh road in Calais Street. This was probably a ritual burial object, as was the cruciform Saxon brooch found near Station Field. Half a 'puddingstone' quern used for grinding corn and brought by the Romans from Hertfordshire was recently found in a field near the brook below Hagmore Green, suggesting there was already settlement there and small farmsteads in that area. For superstitious reasons the practice was to break and discard the quern stone when it was worn out or the woman of the house died. Other smaller fragments of Roman quern stones have been found in the parish, including one found when the road up Sand Hill was widened.

In Roman and Saxon times the area was increasingly settled and the woodlands on the plateau were gradually cleared. Trackways developed following the drier, higher, level ground. The ancient route from Ipswich and Hadleigh to Sudbury wound from farm to farm across the plateau via what is now Hadleigh Heath, Bower House Tye, Tills Farm and Calais Street. It then sought out the easiest place to cross the River Box, descending the spur of land down Sand Hill into the valley and across the brook from Groton at Ash Street. The obvious route across the River Box itself was at a shallow section where it could easily be forded, and where the quite steep-sided valley higher upstream opens out. The reasonably dry rising ground at the foot of what is now Swan Street and Church Street would have given easy access to the ford. This avoided having to cross the broad, marshy section of valley floor downstream which is now crossed by the A1071. From the ford the route led easily up the hill to the drier plateau and on to Newton and Sudbury.

The trackway from Roman Colchester and Nayland to Lavenham and the growing settlement at Bury St Edmunds descended Brick Kiln Hill at Stone Street to follow the western edge of the valley floor to the ford. Again this was the easiest place for it to cross the river and it formed a crossroads here with the east–west route before ascending Swan Street. This crossroads at the ford and the plentiful water supply meant that it was an obvious place for a settlement to grow and for trading to take place, as it still is today.

2
THE EARLY MEDIAEVAL PERIOD
450–1086

THE pagan Anglo-Saxons migrated to Suffolk from southern Denmark and north-east Germany in the fifth century. They spread out and settled, dispossessing the former inhabitants. They too preferred the drier sandy and gravel soils, such as those found along the slopes either side of the Box valley, to the heavier, harder-to-work clays above. Around 570 it is thought that Suffolk, with Norfolk and part of Cambridgeshire, became an independent kingdom of the East Angles, possibly under King Wuffa, who may have been a real historical figure. Christianity was re-introduced in the 630s and missionary centres and monasteries were quickly established. Whilst there is no documentary evidence about Saxon Boxford, it will have been a period of considerable woodland clearance for farming of animals and crops, with the establishment of field systems, small clusters of cottages and land boundaries. In 1002 the River Box was still called the Amulburn.

During this period land holdings became clearly defined and the feudal system began to develop. Bequests through wills of land to the wealthy Abbey of St Edmund in Bury increasingly led to the delineation of parish boundaries locally. In the late Saxon period our parish became demarcated using the existing field boundaries to enable the collection of tithes by the Catholic Church. In the case of Boxford there seems to have been some kind of religious shrine on the present church site during Saxon times. In the ninth and tenth centuries or earlier, this probably evolved into a small wooden church.

THE NORMAN CONQUEST

We have no way of knowing our villagers' reactions to the aftermath of William the Conqueror's victory at Hastings on 14 October 1066. We may imagine, weeks or months later, small groups of Norman soldiers on horseback appearing on surrounding hilltops. They may have sent down outriders into the village to negotiate with the inhabitants. Alternatively they may have just gone past the cluster of hovels around the wooden church, crossed the ford and set up their temporary motte and bailey stronghold at Pytches Mount in Groton, just outside the village. What is certain is that the manor of Groton in which it stands belonged to the Abbey of Bury St Edmunds by 1086. We can surmise that the man hours expended in raising that amount would not have been put in by the Normans themselves, but most likely by the local population acting under extreme duress. The villagers must have soon worked out for themselves their true position under these new oppressors. These must have been hard times for them, regardless of status.

The Little Domesday Survey of 1086 of Suffolk was carried out by the Normans to improve administration and the collection of taxes. It included Boxford, not by name, but as the manor of Kodenham, apparently an outlier of the manor of Cavendish. The other main manor of Boxford, Peyton manor, was founded later. The location of the manor of Kodenham, later known as Coddenham Hall, was on the higher, drier ground north of Hagmore Green. There are no remains of the original manor house and the present Coddenham Hall, close by the A1071, is not on the original site. There would also have been a small cluster of cottages gathered around the wooden church with its twenty acres of 'glebeland' (land used to support the parson) on the south side of the shallow gravel ford, in what is now Church Street and Stone Street Road. Settlement would soon have pushed onto the northern side of the ford along Broad Street and up the rough track (today's Swan Street) along the parish boundary between Groton and Edwardstone. There were also dispersed farmsteads on the higher, drier ground elsewhere in the parish.

In 1086 Boxford consisted of a community of around 100 people, putting it in the largest 40% of settlements recorded in Domesday. By then around 80% of the land was in use and it is estimated that there were around ten landholders per square mile in south Suffolk — at that time the most densely populated area of England.

Most of the land was the responsibility of Ralph de Limésy, Lord of the manor of Limésy in Normandy, an absentee Anglo-Norman magnate and tenant-in-chief of King William the Conqueror. The rest was under Roger of Rames, lord and tenant-in-chief of King William the Conqueror. His home was Rames Castle near Le Havre, Normandy. The total households listed in the Domesday survey consisted of two 'freemen', eight 'villagers', twenty-one 'smallholders' and eight 'slaves'. Freemen and villagers were small-scale landowners, usually with around thirty acres and two oxen. Smallholders would have around five acres and a share in the village plough-team. Slaves (serfs) owned no land and belonged to the lord. They went with the land, but could not be sold. They worked long days on designated strips of land, six days a week, and often barely had enough food for their families to survive. However, in Boxford the survey shows that the vast majority of inhabitants had some land of their own on which they could rely.

An indication of the relative success of the village in 1086 was that it had five lord's plough-teams and four-and-a-half men's plough-teams to work the land, together with twenty-four cattle, fifty pigs and 110 sheep. Usually pasture was not recorded. Other resources included a meadow of ten acres, one mill, thirty acres of church lands and two churches. One was probably the small 'Neeling Chapel' also known later as Peyton Chapel, close to Peyton manor. This was a private chapel, open to parishioners, where prayers would have been offered for the Peyton family.

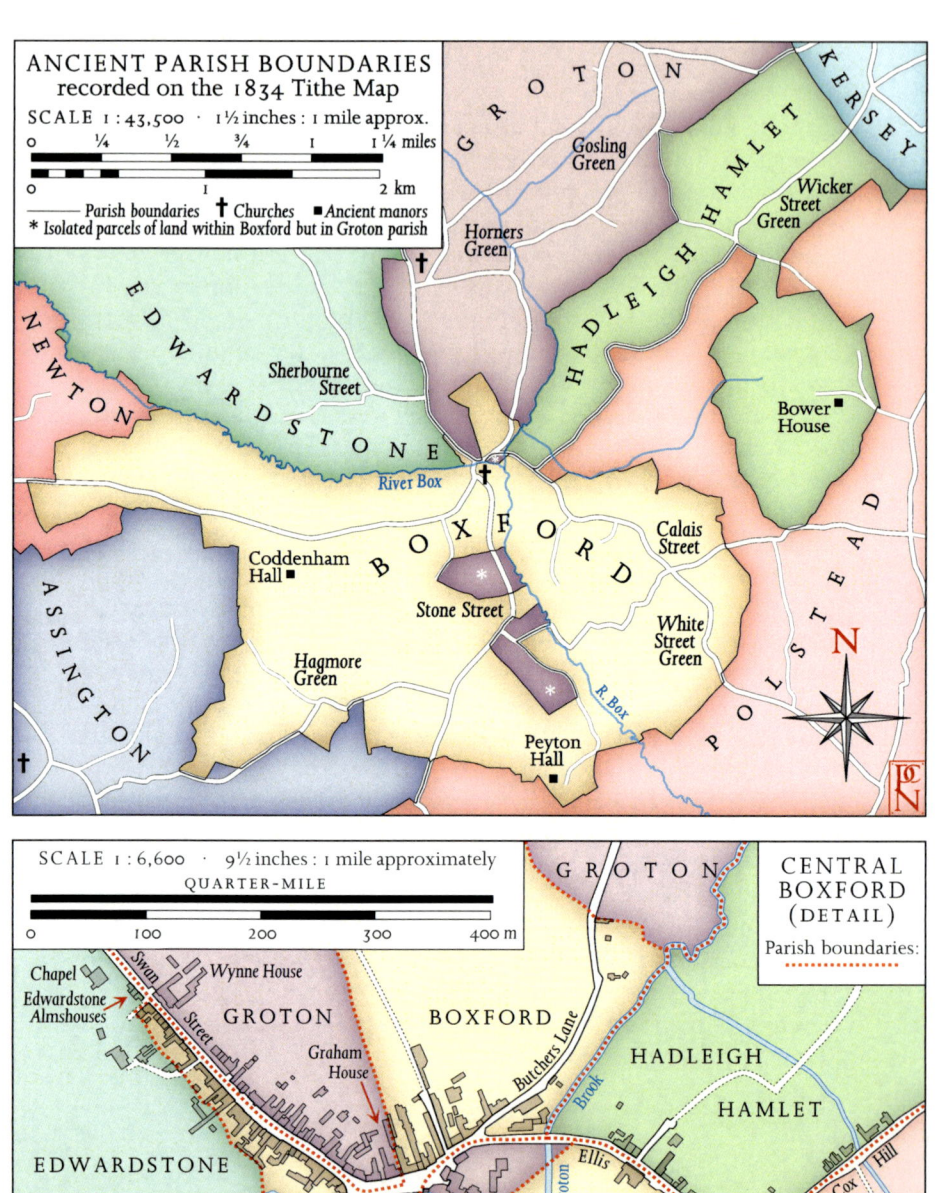

ANCIENT PARISH BOUNDARIES
recorded on the 1834 Tithe Map

SCALE 1 : 43,500 · 1½ inches : 1 mile approx.

0   ¼   ½   ¾   1   1¼ miles

0   1   2 km

—— Parish boundaries † Churches ■ Ancient manors
* Isolated parcels of land within Boxford but in Groton parish

GROTON

KERSEY

Gosling
Green

Wicker
Street
Green

HADLEIGH HAMLET

Horners
Green

NEWTON

EDWARDSTONE

Sherbourne
Street

Bower
House

River Box

BOXFORD

Calais
Street

Coddenham
Hall ■

Stone Street

White
Street
Green

POLSTEAD

ASSINGTON

Hagmore
Green

R. Box

N

Peyton
Hall
■

SCALE 1 : 6,600 · 9½ inches : 1 mile approximately
QUARTER-MILE

0   100   200   300   400 m

GROTON

CENTRAL
BOXFORD
(DETAIL)

Parish boundaries:

Chapel
Edwardstone Almshouses

Swan Street

Wynne House

GROTON

BOXFORD

HADLEIGH

Graham
House

Butchers Lane

Brook

HAMLET

EDWARDSTONE

Ellis

Cox Hill

Groton Brook

Street

N

R. Box

POLSTEAD

River Box

St Mary's
Church

White Hart Inn in
Groton detached

Sand Hill

B O X F O R D

3
THE MEDIAEVAL PERIOD
1086–1200

AFTER the Norman Conquest, parishes and their landholdings were further consolidated. Across the country the Normans strengthened the feudal system of land ownership and established a rigid social hierarchy. Between 1100 and 1200 lands and manors were granted to individuals to bind them to the King and to improve tax collection. As in the rest of south Suffolk, small manors proliferated here, held by rather low-status landlords and characterised by free tenures and a weak manorial structure. Although Boxford therefore never had a wealthy and powerful manor with a strong lord, it is likely that the manor of the Peyton Hall was 'gifted' at this time along with at least four lesser manors here too. The lack of records suggests that these had little influence on daily lives. The first of the family of Fitzwalter to assume the Peyton surname was Reginald de Peyton (c.1100–1136), lord of Peyton, Boxford, and son of Walter de Caen from Normandy. He gave lands to the monks at Thetford and 'fee' to the abbey of St Edmund. He also held Peyton manor at Ramsholt and is buried at Stoke by Nayland. It is thought the family were descended from William de Malet, a Norman knight and possibly a half-brother of William the Conqueror.

Peyton manor was established on the extreme southern edge of the parish, far from its parish church and the growing settlement next to the ford. This meant it exercised less control over its inhabitants than others in Suffolk, where a strong manor with its court would usually be established at the centre of the parish. It owned considerable land in Stoke by Nayland too. However, it seems, as we shall see later, that this was also an advantage, leaving its inhabitants freer and more

9

independent. There are no court rolls remaining and it is doubtful if it ever had a manor court or administered justice. In 1495 T. Peyton paid a fee of £14 to the Abbot of St Edmund, which suggests the manor was not wealthy. The direct line of the Peyton family seem rarely to have lived at Peyton Hall after 1492.

After 1100, most new settlement in Boxford would have been rather piecemeal, consisting of isolated farmsteads or small collections of houses forming hamlets near the parish boundary or around the edges of small 'greens'.

THE COMPLICATED HISTORY
OF THE BOXFORD PARISH BOUNDARY

Ecclesiastical parish boundaries were 'frozen' by 1180 and were firmly demarcated by field boundaries, tracks and natural features such as streams. The earliest settlers had shunned the marshy valley bottom of the River Box and preferred the valley sides and higher ground around for farming. The parish boundary had evolved across this farmland from the eighth century, but, as trade grew, the focus of Boxford shifted more and more to the crossing point at the ford.

For at least the next 900 years the four adjacent parishes of Groton, Edwardstone, Polstead and the 'peculiar' of Hadleigh Hamlet had adjoining boundaries which intruded from the north right down into the Box valley and its crossing-point—in other words, into what is today's village and built-up area of Boxford. A more complicated arrangement is hard to imagine, but as a result of landholdings and church rights it was cemented in place from 1180. It was further complicated by the fact that Hadleigh Hamlet was in the Hundred of Cosford and paid various dues to Hadleigh parish, while the other four parishes were in the Hundred of Babergh. The parish boundaries of Boxford remained cemented like this for over 700 years, as the map on page 8 shows, based on the 1834 Boxford tithe map. They have only been rationalised from this confusion to their present form in the last 140 years, mainly in 1885 and 1934, but finally in 1974.

In the early years Boxford would have been in the shadow of the adjacent parishes. In 1327 it is estimated from taxation records that

Boxford's population was 113 persons, whereas Edwardstone had a population of 128 and Groton 162. In time Boxford assumed pre-eminence because of its location at a crossroads and ford, with ample water and water power which supported the cloth industry. Edwardstone and Groton gradually became satellite settlements of Boxford and the idiosyncratic parish boundaries would cause difficulties and disputes for centuries. As we shall see, this confusion would also be exploited by villagers for the advantages it brought.

On the north side of the river, Boxford parish included only a narrow strip of land and buildings on the west side of Swan Street, up as far as today's Edwardstone almshouses. Beyond and behind was the parish of Edwardstone right down to the river, including the shared watermill and millpond. The mill stood on the site of the present day Mill Surgery and was destroyed by flood and fire in 1934–5. Groton owned the whole of the east side of Swan Street and the Homefield right down into northern Broad Street: as far as, but not including, the Fleece. Lower Butchers Lane and the rest of Broad Street were in Boxford as far as the bridge over the Groton brook at the bottom of present-day Ash Street. Beyond this brook, known in the past as Dyehouse Ditch, land and buildings along the north side of Ellis Street and the west side of Cox Hill belonged to the parish of Hadleigh Hamlet. The east side of Cox Hill and the old court house and police station were in Polstead parish.

The peculiar of Hadleigh Hamlet was completely detached from Hadleigh and remained a distinct parish in its own right until 1934, when it was divided up between Boxford and Kersey. The term 'peculiar' requires some explanation. It seems to have been an Anglo-Saxon gift of land to the Archbishop of Canterbury by Æthelflæd (c.870–918), lady and ruler of the Mercians. She was the eldest daughter of Alfred the Great. The parish always had a very small population. Over time, not surprisingly it looked to Boxford, and came increasingly under its influence when it suited it.

All through the centuries there was friction over tithes, rates and other dues between Boxford, the Hamlet and Hadleigh itself. Several times they took Boxford to court and the Boxford Parish Book for

11

1718–1883 records at Michaelmas in 1778 that 'the occupiers and farmers [of Hadleigh Hamlet] resolved to have no further connection with the Town of Boxford and to make their own rates and to maintain their own poor.' However, it also records that 'the poor of Hadleigh Hamlet have acquired settlement in Boxford and have partaken of all charities.' It also says that the inhabitants attended Boxford church and that over the previous century tithes were paid to the rector. Hadleigh's mayor and parish had made attempts to regain these and it seems likely that disputes continued until the Hamlet's demise in 1934.

Until the nineteenth century Groton also owned a completely detached enclave around the White Hart in Broad Street and two more along Stone Street. It was only in 1974 that the current Boxford boundary was fixed and Whitestreet Green was given to Polstead. This complex juxtaposition of five parishes clearly led to all kinds of disputes, particularly over taxes. It also had advantages for the inhabitants. Land and property in the settlement was spread across the different parishes and manors, weakening control. This increased the freedom and independence of the inhabitants to trade and farm as they wished. It also made Boxford a good refuge for 'escaped' villeins and serfs from other communities to settle in relative freedom. Here they traded around the ford offering food and bed, stabling of horses and working as smiths and carpenters.

4
THE MEDIAEVAL PERIOD
1200–1349

ETWEEN 1200 and 1349 the church and the manorial system (in which landholders provided land to tenants in exchange for their loyalty and service) still held Boxford in their grip, limiting its growth and prosperity. However, evidence suggests the population grew gradually and may have doubled between 1086 and 1348, when it peaked. This may partly have been the result of a steady economic improvement in farming over this period, aided by a 'warm' climatic period when temperatures were about one degree higher than in the twentieth century.

The Abbot of the Benedictine Abbey of St Edmund at Bury was 'the chief manorial lord of the vill of Boxforde' which included the church, twenty acres of land, two acres of pasture and two acres of meadow — the Boxford glebeland. In the Pinchbeck Register of 1286 Boxford is mentioned as paying dues to the Abbot of Bury. Thirty-two Boxford tenants held land belonging to the Abbot of Bury and some paid only one clove for the privilege! Spices were so precious they were often used as currency. About thirty-two others paid dues for subletting land from their immediate manorial overlords. The Abbot provided for the church and he was the principal landowner.

In 1286 the first named clergyman for Boxford was Ralph, the parson, but Jocelin de Brakelonde, a Benedictine monk at Bury Abbey, mentions one here in 1190 in his Chronicle. He was supported by the churchwardens, who were village leaders appointed to maintain the church and the clergy and to collect a tithe (tenth) of earnings from everyone. The Boxford church records began in 1303, but sadly they no longer exist for this early period. They recorded births, marriages and deaths, important events and the churchwardens' accounts for

13

maintenance of the church and its properties. By 1291 Ralph, the parson, was claiming fishing rights illegally in the taxation roll!

BOXFORD PEOPLE'S LIVES IN THE THIRTEENTH CENTURY

Unfortunately no documentary evidence has survived from the people who lived here then. However, recently historians have used the records from other similar southern-Suffolk villages, each with several weak manors like ours, to provide a picture of the economic structure and lives of the inhabitants. Our manors were small, probably less than 120 acres, and sometimes possibly much less. They were of low value and low status, often with absentee owners. They therefore exercised little control over their tenants.

Most Boxford people could not be described as subsistence peasants, but rather as freemen or 'free tenants', because they were not tied strongly to their landlord and any surplus they produced could be sold. They were rent-paying tenant farmers who owed little or no service to the lord. They had a good degree of security of land tenure and independence. They would have needed at least ten to fifteen acres to provide for their families and to pay rent and taxes. In good years they could produce a surplus of barley or wheat for sale, so that they could buy goods they could not produce themselves. They had a strong incentive to farm well and produce as much as possible from their rented arable land, garden and orchard.

Lower down the social order would have been a number of smallholders who rented only a small amount of land. They would also need to earn wages through farm work, crafts or domestic service. Only a small number of people were completely landless. These were 'unfree' labourers (villeins or serfs) who had to work full-time for a landowner or tenant in return for physical and legal protection and the right to work a separate small piece of land for their own basic needs. They would have rented from the landowner a small, one-roomed single-storey home with holes for windows and doors. These were built largely of sticks and straw, sometimes reinforced with mud or manure and supported by poles. Straw had the advantage of being good insulation and easily available after harvest, but highly flammable. So poorly constructed was their flimsy home that it would need constant repair and frequent rebuilding. Only the landowners and wealthier tenants would have had a solid timber-framed building, albeit a single storey with wattle-and-daub panels (a mixture of mud, straw and manure) and a thatched roof.

Such a social system was economically delicately balanced, and bad weather and crop disease or a series of poor harvests could be devastating for everyone. Only the manor would likely have had the reserves to get through such events comfortably. Life expectancy was around twenty years due to the very high infant mortality, but some adults on a good and plentiful diet would have lived into their early fifties. At best, the diet of the serf would have been founded on pottage (a thick soup or stew made by boiling vegetables, grains, and, if available, meat or fish), bread, sprats, oysters, fruit, coarse cheese and thin home-made ale. The ale would have made the water safe and palatable to drink. They would have eaten meat very rarely.

THE FARMING SYSTEM AND SETTLEMENT PATTERN

Forget your school history here, for south Suffolk and Boxford never used the 'open-field' or 'three-field system' which consisted of communally organised, individual peasant holdings of scattered strips in a few large fields belonging to the manor. Although used elsewhere in England, this system was inefficient and led to poor crop yields and low productivity. Under it everyone was forced to conform to village norms of cropping, harvesting and building, and it involved wasting time in travelling from one strip to another to work.

Boxford folk were mainly free tenants with more consolidated land holdings and greater freedom to farm productively, although they almost certainly swore 'fealty' (loyalty) to the Abbot of St Edmund. Many lived in small, dispersed clusters of cottages and farmsteads close to their land. These gathered around small greens: Hagmore Green, Whitestreet Green, Calais Street and Stone Street. 'Street' may have referred to a narrow strip of land along the lane, used like a green for common grazing. This agreed communal designation of greens of shared pasture meant that, from the tenth century, Boxford freemen could enclose their own land when and how they pleased. Therefore the actual settlement was not strongly nucleated and its inhabitants were spread across the parish. During this time the familiar rolling plateau farmland of today would largely have been laid out, with its field pattern of ancient, irregular enclosure, bounded by hedgerows and ditches and a network of narrow winding lanes and paths. This Mediaeval landscape would be readily recognisable to the modern eye.

There may have been some outlying farmed parcels or 'strips' in a few larger fields, but for the tenants the most important land was that near their homes. They would have practised mixed farming. The main crops would have been wheat, barley and a small amount of rye grown for home use, and for local cash sale and consumption when output permitted. Oats were grown for fodder, especially for horses. Beans and peas helped fix nitrogen in the soil and maintain its fertility. The amount of time land was rested under fallow varied, but there was usually some sort of crude crop rotation. Very little cropping would have been organised communally in Boxford, but the rights to graze the fallow and stubble would have been.

Some of the pasture would have been used for hay, essential for winter feed. Farm animals were much smaller and less healthy and productive than those today, as selective breeding had not yet begun. A fully grown bull was slightly larger than a young animal today. Dairy cattle were the most important, grazed on valley meadows and roadside verges. Other livestock included sheep, pigs, cows, goats and chickens. Farmers made their own bread, butter, cheese and ale. In this period oxen were being replaced by horses, which were usually jointly owned and formed communal plough teams.

The greens of common pasture were often small, only one or two acres, with cottages around their margins. Grazing rights were usually attached to the landholdings and cottages adjoining the pasture. The number and types of animal were carefully regulated. Woodland was scarce and patchy, but it was a vital resource, carefully conserved and regulated too. There would have been no 'wild-wood' or original woodland left in our parish by 1086. What woodland there was would have occupied less than 10% of the land. It would be intensively managed and coppiced every five to twenty years for poles, fencing, wattle-and-daub and firewood. Pigs would have grubbed in it. The hedgerow and isolated trees, mainly elm and oak, provided larger timber beams and planks for building. These trees would have been allowed to grow for 25 to 200 years. It has been estimated that the average late-Mediaeval house, such as those built in Boxford during the period of the wealthy cloth industry, could have required up to 200 small trees. By 1327 Suffolk was one of the most populated, intensively farmed and economically advanced areas of England, and much of the woodland would have been converted to arable farming.

Farming methods and limited technology meant that only in good years would there have been surpluses for sale. In years of bad harvest people will have suffered severe hunger and deprivation, relying on the communal working of their lands to survive. This was a period of more equable climate which helped farming, and also of technical improvements. The more powerful horse replaced the ox with the invention of the horse collar and shoe. With the new mould-board plough farmers were able to increase output and improve drainage.

After 1200 the population grew rapidly and from 1280 it outgrew the capacity of the land to provide subsistence, even in good years. It at least doubled between 1086 and the 1340s, when the population peaked. Inheritance meant land was shared out across the sons of each family, resulting in ever smaller landholdings of less than ten acres. Land was subdivided and, in desperation, sold, making matters worse. This pressure resulted in cultivation of the greens and woodland and thus their loss. By 1300 up to 70% of the land would have been arable. A high input of labour and manure would have been needed to maintain food output. By then most villagers, regardless of status, would have been poor, and life would have been precarious. After that year Crown taxes and soaring grain prices added to this downward spiral and made survival the main aim.

The fall in production from the land in the late-thirteenth and fourteenth centuries is illustrated by the gradual decline in the Rector's income. Nevertheless, in 1341 he is shown to have taken a ninth part of the produce of the whole parish in corn, hides and lambs. He also had a dwelling-house with outbuildings, twenty acres of farmland, three acres of meadow, three acres of alder carr, fixed rents, tithes of hay and fruit and three mills. 'Lesser tithes' on the inhabitants included milk, cheese, calves, pigs and eggs. In addition he received expected 'offerings' from the parishioners on days of penitence, feast days and anniversary masses. The Rector clearly had a very comfortable life and healthy income compared with those of most of his parishioners!

MARKETS AND SELLING PRODUCE

Evidence from family names in Boxford in 1327 shows that the village was already specialising in clothmaking. Boxford clothiers were selling their broadcloth in Colchester by 1340. There were already butchers in the village, probably in a 'shambles' where the post office now stands. This is where the animals would have been slaughtered and the meat sold. The main produce for sale at this time was corn, hides and lambs. Boxford was never granted a 'market charter'. This would have required an application by the lord of the manor, but our lord was not resident most of the time. Anyway the Abbey at Bury was known to stifle other markets to enhance its own.

Nevertheless Boxford must have had a market of some sort by the eleventh century because of its location and distance from other significant trading settlements. Perhaps this was another example of Boxford showing its independent spirit. It certainly had a least two regular trade fairs at various times and these could last for three days. They seem to have been held on today's Broad Street. One was on Easter Monday and the other on 21 December, the Feast of St Thomas and winter solstice, and a day of great significance in pre-Christian times. In 1595 and 1596 Adam Winthrop of Groton gave his wife ten shillings and fifteen shillings respectively to go to the fair in Boxford, which illustrates his relative wealth. (10s. was the equivalent of £90 today.) It is unlikely to have been spent on fripperies though. The Easter fair was at its peak in 1705, but by 1793 the Universal British Directory dismissed it as 'not being worthy of notice'.

Records show that in the fifteenth century Boxford people visited 'Steresbrigge' Fair in Cambridge to buy church equipment, wines, spices and delicacies. Stourbridge Fair was a large Mediaeval fair held on the large common that still lies between the Newmarket Road and the River Cam, behind the Leper Chapel as you enter Cambridge from the east. It is thought to have been the largest trade fair in Europe at that time. It started in 1199, when King John granted the nearby Leper Chapel dispensation to hold a three-day fair to raise money to support the lepers. By 1589 the fair was enormous and lasted from 24 August to 29 September — over a month, fitting well between harvest and ploughing. This must have been some event for anyone to want to make that journey on potholed, muddy or dusty, unmade tracks on horseback or waggon.

In the absence of an active governing manor, control of Boxford fairs would have been devolved to the church and gilds. Any remaining fair would have been abolished by the Fairs Act in 1871, the purpose of which was to end the 'grievous immorality' associated with them. It is clear that the clergy were not always the upright, celibate citizens one might assume. Towards the end of the twelfth century Gerald of Wales wrote (in Latin still) that the English village priest had his 'hearth girl', a wife in all but name, 'who kindled his fire, but extinguished his virtue'. His contemporary, Pope Innocent III, claimed this *risqué* book to be his favourite bedtime reading! Clergy bastards and 'nephews' were commonplace, and in some Suffolk parishes there are vivid accounts of the sexual expectations and appetites of the monks of Bury Abbey when they came on 'holiday'. It seems that celibacy was not a prized virtue. A contemporary writer, Walter Map (1140–c.1210), described the habits of the priesthood as 'tavern-haunting, brawling, licentiousness and fathering children'. Not much changed over the following century if we are to believe the poetry of Geoffrey Chaucer (1343–1400).

We do not know if the rector of Boxford led such a life, but there would have been no pews in the nave and celebrations of all sorts were held there at this time. There was no shortage of inns here either. 'Church ales' were a social gathering held frequently in the nave of the church before the Reformation. They were the chief means of raising money for it. There were five or six a year and much food and drink was involved, with music and dancing. In 1535 a play was staged in the church to raise funds, bringing visitors from numerous villages. The biggest and best Ale with supper was always held on Plough Monday, the first Monday after the twelve days of Christmas. The 'Boy Bishop' celebrations and the frequent holiday Ales on saints' days all came to an end with the Reformation, although the twice-yearly trade fairs continued.

THE GREAT FAMINE OF 1314–1317

As we have seen, life here was already precarious before the Great Famine struck. Boxford would have suffered greatly during these years, which began with two years of cold weather and high rainfall. It affected the whole country but hit eastern England particularly hard. Suffolk manorial court records describe floods, drowned livestock and ruined harvests for several years running. The resulting scarcity of basic foods and salt led to high prices and hunger. In some places the lords hoarded grain while the poor starved. The weakness of the manors in Boxford may have at least saved the people from this.

It is thought the famine killed between 5% and 10% of the population in England and reached its peak in 1317. It was followed by the Great Bovine Pestilence that was caused by the 'murrain'—a Mediaeval word for an infectious disease in cattle, possibly anthrax. In 1319–20 it killed around 62% of all cattle. This had a dramatic effect on the supply and price of milk and meat for years to come and therefore the amount of protein that Boxford people could eat. Mortality would have been high from the resulting weakened immune systems. As if this were not misery enough, it was then followed by several years of drought and low crop yields lasting until the early 1330s. Even though output had probably recovered by the 1340s, the people of Boxford would have been in no fit state to resist the Black Death when it arrived in 1349.

5
THE LATE MEDIAEVAL PERIOD
1349–1450

IN 1349 the Black Death arrived for the first time and devastated the national population as well as Boxford and the surrounding villages, probably killing around half of the population. Recent research shows that the valley of the Stour and its tributary, the Box, were an early and major pathway for the arrival of the 'pestilence', which we now know was the bubonic plague. Our thriving coastal trade with London was probably the source. This disease was highly virulent, infectious and lethal with no previous epidemic to provide some immunity. Records show that terrified communities knew it was coming. Suffolk manorial and church records show that nowhere escaped its grip. There was a 60% death rate for priests in this diocese. The epidemic lasted about three to four months in each village, with a devastating effect on the population. In Little Cornard records show that twenty-one families were completely wiped out.

After it had passed, there was immediately a major loss of food production and income from the now neglected land. Landlords were often unable to find heirs for their tenancies and had to waive the service bond of villeins to get anyone to take them up.

There was a further outbreak in 1361 which killed around 10% of those remaining, especially children. At least five more outbreaks occurred over the next hundred years, although only that of 1479 was severe and widespread. As well as the village itself, the outlying clusters of cottages around the greens would have been severely depopulated, and many farmsteads abandoned. No trace of these is found today, as cottages built mainly of poles, sticks and straw would rapidly have decayed. Later piecemeal enclosures and the twentieth-century removal of hedgerows and enlargement of fields would have further obscured any evidence of this disaster.

With the loss of half the labour force many things changed. There was a severe shortage of people to farm the land, and those that were left were unable to work all of it. Much more land was neglected or was used less intensively as pasture, mainly for sheep. The climate was deteriorating and the land was less productive because it could not be farmed as intensively as before. There was some further piecemeal enclosure of land, but the pressure on the scarce woodland was reduced. By the 1360s the landlords and church still found it difficult to find labour for their lands and their tax revenue was greatly reduced. Landowners, desperate for workers to harvest their crops, began offering higher wages to anyone who would work for them. Land was cheaper and labour dearer, changing the balance of power between landlord and tenant. Agricultural workers had rising expectations and unrest grew as the powerful tried to keep things exactly as they had been.

Peasants were, for the first time, able to offer their services to the landowner who would pay the highest wage. The Crown and Church were not happy about this and thought they could return to the feudal past. They tried to hold down wages by statute and fined those who accepted the higher wages offered. This led to a growing sense of injustice and outrage amongst our agricultural and artisan workers. The corrupt behaviour of officials made matters worse. Our villagers would have been well-informed through their trading contacts and had a higher degree of legal awareness and political consciousness than might be expected.

The Peasants' Revolt started in Essex on 30 May 1381, when a tax collector tried, for the third time in four years, to levy a Poll Tax on everyone, partly to fund the King Richard II's wars. Since the Black Death people had become increasingly angry about their fixed and lowly status, tied to the land and serving their landlord, church and king. The anger spread rapidly in south Suffolk. The main grievance was Parliament's Statute of Labourers, passed in 1351, which set a maximum wage and stated that people would be punished with prison if they refused to work for that wage. This meant that, despite the demand for workers and the greater availability of land, poor people stayed poor. The law also allowed the lord to stop his villeins (serfs) moving for better wages. In 1371 the Parish Tax was introduced by the Crown, and Suffolk was made to pay a proportionately higher rate than other counties, with some wealthier villages such as ours penalised more than poorer ones.

The Revolt understandably lasted more than a decade, with grievances about social and economic conditions as well as fines and taxation. Whipped up by the preaching of radical priest John Ball, the peasants were demanding that all men should be free and equal with less harsh laws and a fairer distribution of wealth. Some of the better-off, and even some of the clergy, became involved in the cause too, but it was of course the poorest under the feudal system that were suffering most and had the least to lose. The rebels were very active in Sudbury and Bury throughout 1381. There were at least two known rebels from Boxford, but it is not known what happened to them. On 14 June 1381 the rebels captured the then Lord Chancellor, Simon Sudbury, dragged him to Tower Hill and beheaded him. Simon had been born in Sudbury and had helped rebuild St Gregory's church there. His head was taken down from London Bridge, brought to St Gregory's and is still kept at the church. For many rebels, severe retribution followed and hundreds were tried and hanged. Under pressure the King abolished the Poll Tax and promised to abolish serfdom, but it did not happen until nearly 200 years later in 1574, by which time it had largely died out anyway. The Poll Tax was never introduced again until 1990, when the people rebelled again! In many ways the Peasant's Revolt, though painful, was successful.

CHANGES TO LIFE IN BOXFORD, 1400–1500

By 1400 serfdom had probably vanished from Boxford altogether as a result of the changing balance of power over wages and land, with large numbers of free tenants and small, weak manors. This transformed the patterns of landholding as well as the social order. The rigid relationships between peasants, the church and the nobility gradually loosened. This weakened ecclesiastical control and that of the manorial feudal system. Many of the traditional social constraints had gone, and with them the shackles of a feudal society, aided by the weakness of lordship here in Boxford.

With the passage of time, the people that remained after the Black Death could be more enterprising; they were freer to choose whom to work for and could work land more productively for themselves. The many freemen had a greater degree of independence and autonomy and were now able to play a major role in organising the community. Land was much more readily available and work suddenly easy to find. The decline of the manors reduced bonds of work and taxes for ordinary people. With this marked improvement in freedom and living standards came a robust sense of individualism in Boxford.

The lives of the poorest smallholders slowly improved as it became easier for them to earn money and people were better able to feed themselves. Ordinary folk were now able to spend more on food and drink, shunning the coarsest bread, thin ale and bland pottage that had been their staple diet. Our villagers dressed in higher quality clothes and shoes and were more responsive to fashion. This demand set the stage for the rapid growth of the cloth industry and leather trades. It led to more demand for meat, dairy produce, wool and hides at a time when grain farming was becoming less profitable.

Peasants were able to afford better housing and many now lived in longer-lasting, taller and wider cottages built using wattle-and-daub on a timber frame, rather than just poles, sticks and straw. A simple partition might separate the animals or cooking area. Having livestock in your house was something to aspire to—they were stores of wealth, produced goods such as wool and milk or services such as haulage, and helped keep the house warm. People lived with the smell but spent a lot of time outside. However, it is certain that between 1349 and 1450 the population of Boxford grew very little and may even have declined. With a stable population and fewer of them landless, the people in this period were able to hang on to the production gains they had made after 1349.

In farming there was a contraction in the area devoted to crops, and less labour was needed from the much reduced, but stable, population. Land was less well-tended, with weeds, overgrown hedges and ditches. Landlords could not get labour for their land and therefore started leasing it for periods of ten years or more. This enabled the enterprising peasants to become 'yeomen' farmers by acquiring more land. Even though the countryside was less cultivated and managed, the production of high-quality grains, especially wheat for bread and barley for ale, as well as cheese and butter, grew in response to the demands of growing markets and commercialism. Sheep and wool production were not important around Boxford and declined further as demand faded at home and on the Continent for this low-grade wool. By 1500 the Stour valley, including the Box, had become important for beef cattle and dairying. Some land previously arable was enclosed for pasture. Cattle were driven from the North and Midlands for fattening here, and then onward for sale in the by now populous market of south-east England.

Young teenagers could now leave the family home and sell their labour in a range of occupations and trades as well as farming, building their own separate lives. Women could make a significant wage contribution through spinning wool. By 1500 the lowest ranks of lords (gentlemen) and highest ranks of peasants (yeomen) were the most successful at constructing larger landholdings of over fifty acres and sizeable commercial enterprises. The poorer smallholders would still have had less than fifteen acres, but could supplement their income from crafts and wage-labouring for others and, in some years, even produce a food surplus for sale in local markets. Plentiful work and higher wages gave them a better standard of living. Some peasant families nevertheless went, by misfortune, debt or indolence, into a spiral of poverty and destitution. Increased mobility meant that there was less extended family nearby to help them. The increasing popularity of taverns, gaming and sports did not help.

After the Black Death the severe population decline had led to a reduction in the number of houses in the parish, particularly those of low grade, but by the 1440s some of the remaining houses had grown significantly in quality and size. In industrialising villages such as Boxford these timber-framed houses would now often have an upper floor with bedrooms. The social and economic divisions in the village were widening, however, and social tensions grew. By 1500 Boxford was probably dominated by a handful of yeomen farmers, a small number of wealthy clothiers, and possibly a single gentleman farmer of relatively modest wealth. For a further 350 years after 1400, the church, its rector, clerics and churchwardens would nevertheless play a key role in the life and government of Boxford, not always benefitting the lives of the poor. The population of Boxford continued to grow slowly, peaking at around 1000 by the seventeenth century. Such estimates are particularly difficult because much of the Boxford settlement was not within the parish boundary. If anything it is likely that the actual village population was higher by then and similar to that of today.

Boxford's knowledge of the wider world at this time would largely have been acquired by word of mouth through passing traders, drovers, butchers and itinerant friars who visited regularly. It is believed that monks regularly serviced our church before the Reformation and were lodged at what is now Riverhall in Ellis Street. They used a causeway (the origin of the name of the modern road nearby) to cross the river to the church and may have entered via the ancient priest's door on the south side. It is thought the chapel near Peyton Hall might even have been a small monastery, as two fields there are called Upper and Lower Trinity. The friars brought the gospels to the countryside. They were linked to friaries at Clare, Kersey, Stoke by Clare and even a small cell at Edwardstone. The extensive daily round of worship in our church demanded the services of many priests, as well as the Rector.

Civil unrest and religious unorthodoxy had grown out of the previously rigid social and economic structure. After Thomas Sampson of Kersey was indicted for his part in the Revolt of 1381, anti-authoritarianism grew amongst ordinary people in north Essex and the clothmaking villages of south Suffolk. It was linked with anti-clerical attitudes and dislike of 'dishonest priests'. By the early 1420s this

'Lollardy' was firmly established here, showing the independent spirit of the people. There were revolts and disturbances locally in 1413–14, 1450 and 1471. There was an uprising in Hadleigh in 1450 of local textile workers. This was probably linked to Jack Cade's wider rebellion in southern England, when a slump in trade led to a further revolt against bad government and corrupt officials.

Lollards were drawn mainly from the ranks of craftsmen, artisans and the lower clergy. These people were the mainstay of Boxford and as such were quite detached from the manorial order of the times that was common elsewhere. The increasingly commercialised nature of the local economy made the village more receptive to Lollard ideas. One of their aims was to produce a complete vernacular Bible in English for the first time and to break the Church's monopoly on religious knowledge, which the Lollards regarded as one of a number of injustices perpetuated by the Roman Catholic Church. The re-forming zeal of the Lollards was particularly focused on what they saw as endemic church corruption. Pre-dating the printing press, lack of literacy and the difficulty of disseminating information ultimately led to their failure. That and the punishment, after a brief 'trial', of being burnt to death in an old disused chalk pit in Norwich!

GILDS IN BOXFORD

Boxford's gilds were an important part of the social, economic and religious life of the village for centuries. In Boxford a will of 1622 refers to four, dedicated to St Peter, St John, St Christopher and the Holy Trinity, but religious gilds existed here as early as the thirteenth century. Their flowering offered a spiritual insurance policy as well as loans and social activities in a time of high mortality and frequent epidemics. These were fraternal 'civic' gilds, not restrictive, specialised craft gilds. Their chief function was to provide for the souls of their members, and the gild of St John had its own chapel in a corner of our church.

Gilds organised funerals and supported and prayed for men and women in adversity. Each arranged an annual feast on its patron saint's day, and plays and celebrations, often in the church. The parish and the gild were fundamentally different. The parish was the administrative and pastoral unit of the Catholic Church which levied taxes on its inhabitants. Gilds were local, self-regulating and open to members, both men and women, in the four adjoining parishes. They became very important with the rise of the cloth industry in the fourteenth and fifteenth centuries. They built social and commercial bonds between villagers. They gave all their members a role in regulation and helped the village to function as a community, supporting the poor.

The gilds were already in decline as the cloth industry reached its peak around 1500. The cloth industry and the gilds continued into the seventeenth century, but the growing economy based on money and markets rewarded individual enterprise and here it was the merchants who came to dominate. Under this new regime our craftsmen probably became waged labourers. There is no evidence that our gilds were ever organised around the crafts of weaving, dyeing and fulling.

Later on the gilds' use of the church for secular purposes was frowned upon and a particular room in the village would be shared between the various gilds. We do not have evidence of where this was in Boxford, but the Fleece in Broad Street and the Chequers in Church Street are the most likely places. Gilds were in theory dissolved under an Act of 1547 because they were thought to 'misappropriate godly endowments' for social purposes. This seems to have been ignored in Boxford as there were certainly still four of them in 1622. It is likely the gilds were too important to the independent-minded people of Boxford and their cloth trade.

6
BOXFORD'S GOLDEN AGE
1450–1600

WEALTH FROM THE CLOTH INDUSTRY

BETWEEN 1200 and 1400 the making of woollen cloth was a
very loosely organised 'home' or 'cottage' industry in Suffolk,
as elsewhere. During this period the demand for cloth and raw
wool for export meant that the number of sheep farmed all over England increased significantly. After the Black Death in 1349, much land
could no longer be cultivated by the diminished workforce and was
given over to intensive pastoral farming and profitable wool production instead. The remaining arable farming was moderately intensive too. Compared with the rest of the country, Suffolk was therefore
a reasonably wealthy, densely populated county. This was the foundation for the local growth and success of the cloth trade over the
next two centuries.

Suffolk sheep produced a short, curly wool which was only suitable
for a heavy, felted cloth. At this time much wool was exported as fleeces to Europe to meet the demand of weavers in Flanders and Italy.
Merchants from those places would probably have included Boxford
in their travels. It is often said that skilled Flemish weavers brought
the industry to south Suffolk but, although they arrived in Norfolk in
1330, there is no evidence that they brought the cloth trade to Boxford at this time. Cottage production of broadcloth was already well
established. It was the demand, first for raw wool, and later mainly
cloth that built strong links with the Continent and brought new
ideas, methods and the demands of changing fashions. Boxford weavers were quick to spot shifts in fashion and adapt. Successful commerce encouraged anti-authoritarian and nonconformist behaviour,

self-help and an entrepreneurial spirit. By 1400 the growing demand at home and abroad from the lower orders for dyed clothing and bedding was met by the rapid development in Suffolk of a good-value cloth at competitive prices. By this time cloth had replaced raw wool as the main export, and between 1390 and 1460 cloth production increased fourfold in Suffolk.

For 300 years after 1400 the main English cloth industry was focussed in Norfolk, Suffolk and north Essex. Boxford was part of the very prosperous south Suffolk clothmaking district which included Lavenham, Kersey, Hadleigh, Clare and Sudbury. This was England's leading manufacturing industry at this time. It reached its peak between 1450 and 1550, judging by the wealth and tax revenues it generated. South Suffolk became the wealthiest place in England for a time, outside the few major cities.

WHY DID SOUTH SUFFOLK BECOME SUCH A FOCUS FOR THE CLOTH INDUSTRY?

Historians are generally agreed on the pre-conditions necessary for the concentration of the industry in south Suffolk. These were the proliferation of smallholdings, mainly in the hands of secure free tenants able to supply labour, the high population density and intensive pastoral farming. There were important and specific local conditions here too. The free tenants willingly acquired the necessary skills and were ready and able to work as well as to farm. In the early days Boxford's close proximity to the industries of Bury, Sudbury and Clare meant that ideas and skills were exchanged, helped by travelling merchants passing this way. After 1350 a pool of expertise developed rapidly in Boxford, Lavenham and Hadleigh. There was soon a well-established culture of entrepreneurialism and independence. A few energetic individuals seized on the system of outworking as the market demand grew, and they became clothiers managing the industry. In Boxford they were unhampered by the restrictions of urban gilds and authorities. As a result they found and exploited new markets and fashions, and were able to shift the focus to higher quality cloth when the lower-end market stagnated after 1400.

This area became pre-eminent quite quickly. By 1450 the tax on raw wool for export encouraged the freemen of Boxford, unfettered by the manor, to make better cloth as home and overseas demand was growing. The weak manor, the freedom from a single authority provided by the overlap of our settlement with four other parishes and the declining influence of the Abbey meant our villagers could be entrepreneurial and make the best of these opportunities. The River Box importantly provided a reliable water supply, as large quantities were needed for cleaning the wool, for dyeing and for fulling the cloth. There is no evidence that the development of the fulling mill was important in the growth of the industry here. Relative proximity to the main market and port of export in London was important. Blackwell Hall, adjacent to the Guildhall in the City of London, was the centre for the wool and cloth trade in England from Mediaeval times until the nineteenth century. Clothiers and traders from across England brought their material to Blackwell Hall to display and sell it to merchants and drapers.

THE ORGANISATION OF THE CLOTH INDUSTRY

After 1460 the previously loose domestic organisation of cloth production was replaced by the very effective organisation of structured 'outwork', and marketing now concentrated in the hands of, and managed by, a few 'clothiers'. A few of our most enterprising villagers became such clothiers: clothmakers who organised and controlled the whole process, from funding, buying and transporting the wool, to making it into cloth and selling it. This enabled them to control costs and impose some quality control. This was the key to Boxford's success and these men became very wealthy indeed. Thomas Coo of Boxford, for example, amassed a huge fortune and by the 1520s paid more tax than the rest of the village put together, far more than the manors did. His sons William and Thomas also became wealthy clothiers and churchwardens.

The rise of wealthy local clothiers is illustrated in the ownership of Coddenham Hall manor. In 1316 Thomas Fitz Eustace was the lord of the manor. He was probably an absent nobleman owner. In the

31

fifteenth century it was owned by another absentee, Robert Clopton, who seems to have been an Alderman of London linked to many other Suffolk manors and one at Halstead. However, by 1492 the lordship of Coddenham Hall manor was owned by William Forth, a very wealthy clothier of Hadleigh. After three more generations it passed to William Risbie of Lavenham and in 1655 it was in the hands of another family of rich clothiers, the Brond or Brand family. The Bronds were linked to manors at Polstead, Edwardstone, Great Cornard and Bures. This illustrates how wealth was passed through generations but did not always remain in Boxford itself. By 1885 Coddenham Hall belonged to C. J. Grimwade who lived at Toppesfield Hall, Hadleigh, and he was also linked to manors across Suffolk.

The many processes of cloth production were controlled through outwork from the clothier's warehouse. Better-quality, finer fleeces were brought by packhorse from Lincolnshire, the Essex marshes and the Welsh borders in particular. The fleeces were then 'put out' to women and children in their wattle-and-daub cottages for cleaning, combing and spinning as piecework. The wool was carded or combed out between two wooden boards with fine teeth before it was spun. Much spinning would have been done by distaff and spindle as it was only in the 1550s that the spinning wheel became more common and improved output considerably. The spun wool was then collected and put out again for weaving by men. Large windows in the upper storey facing south-east, along Butchers Lane for example, enabled them to weave on wooden looms from dawn to dusk.

The cloth would then be taken to the river for cleaning and fulling (beating). Fulling removed grease from the cloth using 'fuller's earth', a natural clay containing ammonia salts. This was brought from the Continent by foreign merchants who exchanged it for cloth. It replaced the stale urine which had earlier been used for fulling. The cloth would then be stretched out on tenterhooks to dry. One such place lay upstream from the bridge on the south-facing slope of the valley below Goodlands. Dyeing with woad took place at any stage according to the particular cloth required. Woad was a blue dye obtained from a plant of the cabbage family and it was grown widely for this purpose. Back at the clothier's warehouse the cloth was sheared by shearmen to get rid of the nap and fuzz, and teaselled with a seed head to give it a soft smooth finish. Finally it would be baled and stacked ready for sale and shipment.

Boxford already had well-established access to merchants in London, Ipswich and King's Lynn, and ports and contacts in Continental markets. Between 1519 and 1527 Thomas Howell, a member of the Drapers' Company, one of the London wool companies, sent his agent to Suffolk towns including Boxford to buy cloth, even bargaining for it before it was made. In particular he bought from an important and wealthy Boxford clothier named Symon Newton, who died in 1531. The agent mostly bought broadcloth (a heavy, plain woven cloth), or an even cheaper and coarser Suffolk cloth called 'vesses'. This was cheaper because it was exempt from the normal standards set for broadcloth. The colour of broadcloth was generally blue, either azure or plunket, a light grey-blue. Most of Thomas Howell's cloth was exported to Spain and Portugal. He constantly paid the Suffolk clothiers with 'balles of wood' (bales of woad), and 'boggs of alem' (bags of alum, used in dyeing to brighten colours) and only partly with money. In 1595 Henry Browne left his dyehouse in 'Boxford Street' to his daughter Ann Snelling. This is thought to be next to Peyton House, beside the Groton brook coming down beside modern Ash Street to join the River Box.

The local 'searcher' was an important figure in the industry. He was an appointed quality-control officer who checked the length and quality of each bale before it was sent to the London market. His stamp gave the merchants and buyers confidence. Adam Winthrop was a searcher and gave evidence against Boxford clothiers prosecuted for illegal stretching of the cloth to make the bale appear longer and more valuable. Our clothiers were not the most honest, for between 1524 and 1640 no fewer than sixty-six appeared in legal proceedings.

By 1500 Boxford had specialised and become highly dependent on the export of high quality broadcloth to the Continent. This specialisation meant that Boxford clothiers were less able to adapt quickly to increasing changes of fashion and demand, although this had previously been their strength. This did not bode well for the long-term future of the industry. Probably more than half the Boxford population was by now involved in some way in the cloth industry and most of the rest would have been involved in retail, crafts or services supplying them. This made the village heavily dependent on the trade and vulnerable to any setbacks.

In the meantime this new-found wealth led to a major building boom and Boxford expanded rapidly. The main settlement developed significantly on the northern side of the river where the bulk of it is today, regardless of the boundaries with the other four parishes then. Ancient House in Ellis Street is a good example of one of many large timber buildings put up by the wealthy clothiers at this time, often replacing wattle-and-daub cottages. It was constructed around 1485, mainly from elm rather than oak, probably by Thomas Coo, the clothier. The fact that it was on the north side of Ellis Street and technically in Hadleigh Hamlet shows how integrated the parishes were for commercial activity by this time.

The timbers for Ancient House, some of which were re-used from earlier buildings, were dragged from Lavenham timber yard, where they had first been erected as a frame and each joint numbered for later re-assembly. It was originally a large, tall, L-shaped building with an impressive large hall facing Ellis Street, where №20, Whymark House, is now. The unnecessarily close-spaced timber studs seen in the outside wall today, where this hall joined the service wing of the 'L' of Ancient House, was an ostentatious display of wealth. The studs did not need to be this close together for construction purposes, as wattle-and-daub was the infill, but so much timber on display was evidence that money was no object. The studs of the remaining part of Ancient House facing Clubs Lane are nothing like so close, as this was the original service and warehouse wing. It also contained a kitchen, pantry and buttery for wines and ales, and chambers (bedrooms) for the adjoining hall.

The continuation of Ancient House (№16) away from this service section would have been the clothier's warehouse and workshop for shearing and storing the finished cloth. There would have been a yard, a well and stabling enclosed behind the L. Before the building of the huge brick chimney in the late sixteenth century, supporting the newly inserted upper storey for wool storage, it had a large tall open room with a rare (in Suffolk) smoke bay. This consisted of a large timber and plaster structure which guided the smoke from the open hearth up to a shuttered opening in the roof and kept it out of the rest of the building. This hearth may well have been used for cleaning and dyeing.

BUILDING THE CHURCH OF ST MARY

There is little documentary evidence about the building of the present stone church, but we do know that between 1420 and 1470 a team of Sudbury masons was working on it. The earliest reference to a church in Boxford is found in 1190 in the Chronicle of Jocelin de Brakelonde, a Benedictine monk at Bury Abbey, but it must have existed long before then. The list of rectors goes back only to Ralph, the parson, in 1286. The structure of the present building dates from around 1420 onwards when the cloth industry began to develop rapidly, and with it the wealth of the village. Some inhabitants were very aware of their improved life and achievements and wanted to benefit the community. The reconstruction of the parish church was done through bequests and fundraising out of pride and piety, as well as caring for their own souls in the afterlife. This was community action in an age of growing individualism.

This generosity and wealth, and the extent of individual land ownership, is illustrated by numerous wills. In 1444 John Cowper, a clothier, left nineteen marks (one mark was roughly two-thirds of a pound) in his will to complete and finish the bridge with stone. He also required work on the cross, church porch and bridge to be finished in three years or the money disposed of. In 1451 Thomas Cowpere left a croft of arable land called Longcroft to Joan his wife for ten years and after that to his sons and heirs for ever. In 1461 John Aleyn of Groton left Croft Meadow, then called Lysses Croft, to his wife Joan, land which later became Boxford playing field. Some of the

35

The rare, rib-vaulted, wooden north porch of St Mary's church,
of unknown date, but earlier than the fifteenth-century church itself.

wealthy left money for the upkeep of the 'ways' (roads). In 1491 Agnes Sargeant (still a Boxford surname today) left the 'meadow of Lyn-croft to Boxford Town'. Historians today classify Boxford as a town during Mediaeval times before the rise of the cloth industry, as it had a population of well over 300 people, at least twenty different crafts and trades serving a wide area, social stratification and a degree of self-government.

Other surviving wills between the years of 1438 and 1522 show that the church received rich benefactions, but mainly for ornaments and vestments. This suggests that the church was already substantially built by then. We know that the impressive south porch, built with Caen limestone, was added in 1441 following bequests. This stone was brought on flat-bottomed boats up the River Box and originated in Normandy. This may be hard to believe looking at the river today, but many years ago traces of what was almost certainly a landing place were found on the south bank close to the church. Only 100 years ago the river was much deeper and more reliable in flow. In the late Mediaeval period there may have been more rainfall, water tables were certainly much higher and springs stronger, with fewer people to use it and no pumping and abstraction upriver for farming.

The north aisle of the church was built later. It is not known when the rare, rib-vaulted, wooden north porch was placed against the north wall of the church to decorate another entrance. The structure is fourteenth-century or earlier, certainly older than the fifteenth-century stone church itself and it is not known where it came from. Some have suggested it came from a monastery. It is a remarkable survivor of its type. It is thought by some experts to be the 'most wonderful wooden porch in the country'. In 1465 'John Cowper of Stone' (Stone Street) left money for the vestibule and a lantern on the tower to house a bell. Clearly our clothiers wanted to show their wealth and secure their afterlife.

The church building in the 1500s acted as a venue for church services, gild processions and pageants, as a theatre for mystery plays and a public hall for meetings and church ale parties to raise funds. Thomas Coo, our most wealthy clothier, organised these and the

FLINT & BUTTRESS: THE FASCINATION
OF FIFTEENTH CENTURY CRAFT   BOXFORD CH: Suffolk

W·H CAFFYN
1945.

A 1945 drawing of the west door of St Mary's church by
W. H. Caffyn (1870–1958), Boxford illustrator & artist.

tippling took place in the church. At every service our villagers would have been filled with wonder at the beautiful colours, statues and stories told in the many wall paintings. These scenes from the lives of saints, Bible stories and vivid depictions of Heaven, Hell and Purgatory would have left their imaginations running riot about the Day of Judgement that awaited them. Sadly there is little left of these works of art today.

BOXFORD, 1500–1550

Sometime in the late fifteenth century, a member of the long-standing King family of Boxford, Anne King, was fortunate enough to be asked to become the first wife of Thomas Spring III of Lavenham. He was a clothier and one of the wealthiest men in England, having inherited his business from his father and grandfather. He probably met her on one of his frequent visits to Boxford where he owned land and several houses, probably occupied by his spinners and weavers. This illustrates the high degree of business involvement between the local cloth towns, and Boxford should not be seen as an isolated community at this time. Anne would no doubt have been familiar with the trade and therefore a suitable wife. The wedding was probably a grand affair for a Boxford girl, attended by knights, country gentlemen, clothiers and merchants from London, with days of feasting and merry-making. They went on to have four children. Thomas Spring III married again after Anne's death and his second wife, Alice, inherited in 1523 a piece of land of around one acre lying in what sounds like Broad Street, Boxford, but within the parish of Groton which came down to Broad Street. She also had another piece of meadow that lay either side of the river in Stone Street next to the then rectory, known as the parsonage. These plots are probably the enclaves mentioned earlier and they remained outlying 'islands' of Groton in Boxford until the twentieth century.

In 1523 John, eldest son of Thomas Spring III and Anne, inherited most of his father's wealth and lands. He married the daughter of Sir William Waldegrave, eventually leaving the cloth trade behind and becoming a country gentleman. He helped suppress the Lavenham revolt of 1525 (see below) and removed the bells from the church of St Peter and St Paul in Lavenham, meaning the rebels could no longer be called to arms that way. He was later knighted for his trouble.

Robert Forde the elder, gentleman and 'chief lord' of Boxford, was responsible for preparing the Muster (Military) Roll for Boxford and surrounding villages. This was a list showing those available to serve in King Henry VIII's army. In 1522 the Roll for this parish alone included eleven clothiers, four dyers, two fullers, six shearmen and thirty-seven weavers. Wool workers obviously formed a significant proportion of the growing wage-earning population. There were three more wool workers in Boxford than in its better-known and very wealthy rival, Lavenham. The Muster Roll also records that ninety-one inhabitants were eligible for taxation to help Henry VIII fight his French wars. William Coo, clothmaker, was outstandingly wealthy, assessed for tax on £200 in 'moveables' and £7 in land. He therefore had to provide five harnesses, two bows and two sheaves of arrows and three billies (bill hooks) for the King's French effort. Even Lady Peyton at the Hall was only assessed at £27, whilst the parson was assessed at £50. We can guess that Robert Forde would not have been very popular in the village after this muster! A total population of 416 for the parish has been estimated for this date.

In 1525 Thomas Wolsey introduced a harsh new tax called the 'Amicable Grant'. (It seems that deliberately misleading descriptions of new policies by politicians were already common currency in the sixteenth century.) It was designed to pay for Henry VIII's French wars. This hit a population already heavily taxed by the Muster Roll. For those earning over £50 the new tax was to be 17%, for those between £20 and £50 it was 13% and for everyone else 5%. This would cause great unemployment and poverty throughout the land, and particularly in the prospering cloth-manufacturing towns of south Suffolk. Rebellion broke out and the biggest was in Lavenham where '4000 people assembled and caused the bells to be rung to rouse the district'. The Dukes of Suffolk and Norfolk arrived with a small army and crushed the rebellion, imprisoning the rebel leaders in the Fleet Prison, London. The King quickly decided to back down and claimed that he knew nothing about the Amicable Grant and that he had not authorised it. A general pardon was granted for the rebels. It is certain that the people of Boxford were involved, but names and numbers are not known. It was the first sign that the cloth industry might face harder times ahead.

Boxford is fortunate in that, from 1529 onwards, the churchwardens' accounts have survived. Those for 1530–1561 have been translated by Peter Northeast and published by the Suffolk Records Society. They illustrate the *minutiae* of parish life. Churchwardens had to be 'substantial men' of the parish who had already given some service; for example organising church ales. The Accounts illustrate well the dramatic changes affecting church life and finance during the middle years of the sixteenth century. They show what was the norm in Boxford before the Reformation and the tumultuous years that followed, before the relative tranquillity of the Elizabethan period. The churchwardens' funds came from rents and church dues, but entertainments (ales) were the main source of income. Money was spent on church silverware, candles, vestments and maintenance, and dues to the Pope until Henry VIII stopped these in 1534.

In 1529 the bridge was mended with posts and clay for the sum of 11*s.* 9*d.* (59p). This gives some idea of the value of money at that time and illustrates the weight of the taxes levied by the Muster. In 1530 William Coo is recorded as the transporter of an organ for the church from King's Lynn. The clothiers had substantial carts for transporting their wares and he was paid 21*s.* 4*d.* (£1.07) for the service.

In 1531 Boxford paid rent of 12*d.* (5p) a year on Turks Hall at Hagmore Green to the Knights of St John. This seems to have been an ancient and unusual levy for which our parish was responsible. These Knights Hospitaller were a Catholic military order originally established in Jerusalem in 603 and they became important during the Crusades. After seven years of moving from place to place in Europe, the Knights had settled in Malta in 1530 when Holy Roman Emperor Charles V, as King of Sicily, gave them Malta, Gozo and the north African port of Tripoli in perpetual fiefdom in exchange for an annual fee of a single Maltese falcon.

In 1540 clothmaker John Gaurge left in his will his 'meadow at the fulling mill and the lease of Peyton mill and Newton mill'. Whilst valuable, these did not indicate enormous wealth for this particular clothier.

In 1549 archery butts were built, but we do not know where in the village. A butt is an archery practice field, with mounds of earth to support the targets. Henry VIII had passed an Act in 1511 requiring longbow practice to provide a reserve of men for military service in his army, as he feared that archery was declining as a sport and skill. He ordered that all men under the age of sixty practise archery regularly, and that fathers be responsible for providing their sons and young male servants with archery equipment and training. In 1642 just before the outbreak of the Civil War, a Mr Greene was asked three times to repair the butts. (Archers were used in England for the last time in a siege at the outbreak of the English Civil War in 1642.)

The Dissolution of the Monasteries by Henry VIII between 1534 and 1541 seriously harmed rural England. In confiscating the lands and income of the church, he caused a social crisis. Bury Abbey finally surrendered to his pressure in 1539 and was dissolved. Its wealth was taken over by the Crown. The Abbey had been in decline for some time and had been attacked and burnt by local people several times over previous centuries because of its unfair taxes, but it retained some control over places such as Boxford until 1539. Church lands were then given by the King to the nobility, who often exploited the people even more than the church had done. After the Reformation even the playing of the organ and singing in our church was disapproved of, and in 1644 it was forbidden altogether.

Boxford was initially fortunate that it had income from the cloth trade to protect it somewhat, although this was increasingly taxed and in steep decline. Our clothiers became quite rebellious at the new taxes and the loss of church silver and art which their families had donated. This unrest was effectively quelled by Henry VIII's royalist leader, Thomas Howard, Third Duke of Norfolk, who had a house at Stoke by Nayland. He 'calmed the light young clothiers of Hadleigh and Boxford' by conscripting them into military service. It should be noted that Boxford was always more closely linked in the wool trade to Hadleigh, rather than to Lavenham or Sudbury.

DECLINE

The decline from Boxford's 'Golden Age' really began after 1560 and continued throughout the next century. After 1550 the Tudor government started to exercise control over production and quality, demand for our heavy broadcloth declined, and with it the price. A major factor was Boxford's inability to adapt to the competition from the new lighter cloths now being produced. These 'new draperies' were first developed by Flemish weavers, invited by the government to come and settle in England and practise their trade. The aim was to reduce England's dependence on foreign imports as demand for these new cloths grew. In 1565, the Norwich authorities sent a representative to Queen Elizabeth I, asking for permission for immigrant workers to settle in Norwich, and twenty-four households soon arrived there. They were keen to come because of the persecution of Protestants, the hardship and war in their homeland.

These lighter cloths became very fashionable. The newer, cheaper and better cloths brought by the Flemish weavers made Boxford's old-fashioned broadcloths look poor value. These 'strangers' taught local workers in their area to produce the new types of cloth through apprenticeship, but they never came to Boxford. They did settle in north Essex and one wonders if the wool workers in Boxford were not open to new ideas and skills, despite the falling prices and reduced demand for their own product. Nevertheless, at this time Boxford still had sixty-seven broadcloth weavers compared with only twenty-one in Lavenham. At the beginning of the seventeenth century Boxford clothiers still served on the governing committees of the Bury Corporation of Clothiers, Clothmakers, Weavers and Tailors, a kind of gild. They were obviously important members and the distance of twenty miles on horseback was clearly no object. The purpose of this was to try to counter the monopoly that London held over the foreign export cloth trade. Boxford eventually found itself, at best, only supplying spun yarn to weavers in Norwich and Essex.

By 1676 there is evidence that the clothmaking industry had all but died out. It had collapsed here long before the industrial revolution, with its coal, steam power and factories, relocated the English woollen industry to the West Riding of Yorkshire. The death of the local industry was signalled when, in 1686, Boxford appointed its last searcher for cloth. It is thought that at least 70% of the people of Boxford were employed in the cloth industry at it peak, but by 1700 this figure was probably less than 20%. From then onwards the town lost its significance and relied on a wide diversity of wage-earning occupations that served the village and surrounding area.

RELIEF OF THE POOR

Roaming beggars, vagrants and crime became commonplace in rural areas after the social support of the religious houses was removed during the Dissolution of the Monasteries. Their support for the poor with food and shelter had been essential. The Boxford churchwardens' accounts show that voluntary collection of funds for the poor was already taking place here by 1533 when the Reformation began. Initially nine or ten people were helped with gifts of wood and small amounts of money.

After the Dissolution in the 1530s government became more centralised and the basis of the economy changed from land to money. It made it easier for Boxford farmers to sell surplus produce, but wages of the poor fell and land was scarce. This encouraged the enclosure and consolidation of any remaining unenclosed land and its more productive use, but poor labourers became poorer still with these changes in agriculture. Economic depression and large-scale unemployment followed the decline of the 'old draperies' in Boxford. The decline in the cloth trade and agricultural work affected almost everyone in Boxford as all the trades and labourers were interdependent. Many skilled men took to the roads to find work, leaving their families at home to seek poor relief.

With the Poor Relief Acts of 1564, 1597 and 1601, the parish (or 'vestry' as the village council was then known) was given wider administrative powers with courts and appointed constables. It was

44

given responsibility for poor relief and roads as well as for paying tithes to the now 'English' church. Roaming beggars were targeted and a parish supervisor or 'overseer' of the poor was appointed. The 'deserving poor', unable to work due to illness, disablement or age, were treated very differently from those who 'chose' not to work, the 'idle poor'. Initially the help was given through 'out relief', whereby clothing, food or firewood was distributed to those in need in their own homes and work was provided using flax, hemp or wool. Women and children were sent to pick stones from the fields and place them by the lanes for their men to use in road mending. Poorhouses were increasingly needed and they were usually charitable church or gild foundations.

It should be noted that surnames still familiar in Boxford today are mentioned in the Census of the Poor Register Books of 1597: Baker, Clarke, Gage, Goymer, Kinge, Kingsburye, Salmon and Warde.

Old School House today. The grammar school was founded in 1596 and closed only in the 1880s.

7
GRADUAL ECONOMIC DECLINE
1600–1800

OVER this period, despite accelerating poverty, Boxford town, as it was still called, developed a diverse range of occupations linked to farming, trades, crafts and services. The town was the centre for several surrounding villages and hamlets and provided for their daily needs. Few would have owned a horse and therefore most wants had to be met within walking distance. Visits to market in Sudbury and Hadleigh would have been rare for ordinary folk and goods that could not be made locally would increasingly be brought in by horse and wagon from Ipswich and its port.

At this time the football matches held in Boxford were called 'camping' matches and played with a pig's bladder. These were nothing like today's game. They were often very violent, involved wrestling and were played by large teams over a considerable area of land with few rules. Broken limbs were common, as John Winthrop recorded in March 1617. On 12 September 1750 a camping match was held, probably behind Swan Street, with fancy hats as rewards. The following day a further match was played for less fancy hats. The King's Head in Broad Street and the Fleece delivered the awards to the players, and no doubt much ale as well.

In 1625 Boxford inhabitants were forbidden to harbour vagabonds and were at risk of a fine. There were many people on the roads wandering from place to place without work or a home, some of them ex-soldiers. Villages would always try to push onto the next village any newcomer who threatened to become a financial burden on the parish, and they were often handed from one constable to the next. There were at least two appeals against this practice in Boxford in the eighteenth century. The outcome is not known.

The Pourtracture of the Reverend and worthy Minifter of God,
William Ames D.D. fometime of Chrifts Colledge in Cambridge.
And Proffefor of Divinity in the Famous Univerfity of
Franeker in Friefland .

Will Marfhall fculpfit.

Printed for Iohn Rothwell at the Sunn in Paules Church yard

*William Ames (1576–1633), a pupil of Boxford school, who became a
famous English Puritan theologian, remembered for his writings on
ethics and for debating and writing in favour of strict Calvinism.*

EDUCATION

As early as 1532 a school house was supported by the church in Boxford. Its most famous pupil was William Ames. Ames was born at Ipswich, and was brought up by a maternal uncle, Robert Snelling of Boxford. He went to Christ's College, Cambridge in 1594, graduated with an M.A. in 1601 and was chosen for a fellowship in Christ's College. He was popular and in his fiery sermons he rebuked the 'heathenish debauchery' of the students during the twelve days of Christmas (nothing changes!). William became a puritanical religious man who produced publications which resulted in him having to flee to the Continent. He was known for his theology and was frequently quoted in the colonies of the New World, more often than Calvin and Luther combined. The school sent other boys to Caius College, Cambridge between 1560 and 1576.

THE FREE SCHOOL OF QUEEN ELIZABETH I

In 1596 the grammar school was granted a charter by Queen Elizabeth I through which John Gurdon of Assington provided the land. It occupied what is now the Old School House on School Hill, built soon after 1602. It was required to promote the learning and instruction of the youth of Boxford, Edwardstone, Groton and, eventually, Assington. In the ensuing centuries, endowments and legacies were regularly left to support local boys. Philip Gostlinge and John Snelling, Puritans, were its main founders. Initially, successive Boxford rectors each became Master and they seem to have had strong Puritan leanings throughout the seventeenth century. The thirty-seven governors were also Puritan in inclination and were drawn from the landowning and yeoman gentry across south Suffolk. Some lived five or six hours' ride away and the rare meetings were, not surprisingly, badly attended. Over thirty years there were rarely more than four governors at meetings. From 1632 the school finances and endowments were managed by a voluntary warden on behalf of the governors.

The school funds were very limited and it was always hard to find a qualified Master, who needed to be a Master of Arts in holy orders.

Masters were constantly leaving, as were their 'ushers' (assistant teachers). In the early days there were up to eight pupils, aged eight to fourteen. The carved initials of some of them can still be seen inside Old School House. With a new legacy in 1788, numbers increased to twelve pupils. They were the sons of shopkeepers and tradesmen in the three villages, but specifically not paupers (nor girls for that matter). Places were free, but there was an annual charge of 8*d.* (3½p) for writing materials. Much of the early curriculum would have been Latin grammar, texts and Scripture. Quite late in the school's life English, reading and arithmetic would have been added.

In 1805 the boys and the Master had to attend a governors' meeting for their books, progress and improvement to be examined. In 1829 the Commissioners said that, although the Revd Plume was the master, with no usher, it had 'long ceased to be maintained or attended as a free grammar school'. There must have been some attempt to revive it, as in 1844 White recorded that the endowments were too small for more than eight free scholars, two each from the four parishes, including Assington by this time. White opined that there was 'no demand for dead languages' and the schoolmaster was only required to teach reading, writing and arithmetic.

When Boxford National School opened in Stone Street Road in 1839 it was the death-knell for the grammar school. In 1850 the school house was transferred to the Official Trustees of the Charity Lands, which in turn merged with the other Boxford charities in 1878, in which year an Act of Parliament heralded the introduction of compulsory elementary education from 5 to 13. The grammar school was reconstituted for a few more years but closed for good in the mid-1880s. The building was finally sold in 1906 with a market value of £194. The United Boxford Charities Trust continues to provide annual assistance to individuals with educational needs.

1626: THE GREAT PLAGUE RETURNS TO BOXFORD
The bubonic plague or Black Death was a regular visitor to England over the centuries following 1349. There was a minor outbreak of plague in Boxford in 1602–4, when it was severe in Groton, judging

by the number of burials. It is odd that it did not significantly raise burials in Boxford, since some of the inhabitants of Groton lived opposite them in Swan Street and Broad Street! There was another later outbreak, again minor, in 1664, but the severe plague crisis in Boxford parish was in 1624–6, when large numbers of inhabitants died. Only nine other Suffolk parishes fared worse than Boxford in the seventeenth century. In 1626 there were seventy-four burials in Boxford compared with twenty-eight the year before and nineteen the year after. These figures are those in the church records and there may have been other unrecorded deaths disposed of by burial in the fields.

Church burials show that this visitation of the Plague arrived in Boxford in March 1626. There was no obvious geographical pattern to the spread of plague across the country. In 1625 it appears to have originated in Great Yarmouth, brought by ship from Rotterdam. However, Clare was the first Suffolk parish to suffer, showing its apparently random spread. The rats and fleas which spread it were carried in grain and wool, which was imported for local weavers at this time. Traders could travel up to twenty-five miles a day which might explain jumps in its spread. The plague was generally less virulent nationally in 1626 when Boxford suffered its worst crisis. There were two killer diseases present in the 1626 crisis, however. Both bubonic and pneumonic plague occurred simultaneously, but the bubonic variant was not highly contagious. Both however, could lead to death and frequently did.

In 1664–5 Boxford suffered another plague crisis which came close to being measured as severe. This is nationally known as the Great Plague, for it hit other areas much harder than Boxford, including London, which lost roughly 15% of its population. Epidemics and infectious disease regularly afflicted life in Boxford throughout the ages until well into the twentieth century. It is thought that smallpox was first introduced into Britain by those returning from the Crusades in the eleventh century. In 1689 and 1737 in particular there were severe epidemics of smallpox in Boxford and many died. A 30% death rate was usual. In 1796 smallpox vaccination was developed by

Edward Jenner, but the disease was only finally eradicated world-wide in 1977. 'Spotted fever', now known as typhus, occurred routinely and it struck the village particularly hard in 1691. Poor people with insanitary housing and weak immune systems were the most susceptible to these diseases. The death rate was again up to 30% and in that year a large number of burials and coffins had to be charged to the parish.

Interestingly, the last confirmed bubonic plague deaths in England were at Holbrook, Suffolk, in 1912 and infected rats were found at that time as close to Boxford as Washbrook and in many other places in and around Ipswich.

ST MARY'S CHURCH BELLS

Our church has a fine set of eight bells. The earliest was purchased around 1410, as Boxford began to grow more prosperous from the cloth trade. There must already have been a stone church tower by then in which to hang it. This bell was hung just in time to ring out in celebration of Henry V's famous victory at the Battle of Agincourt in October 1415. This was one of the decisive battles in the Hundred Years' War against France and was a cause of much joyous celebration. It was the English longbow archers that won this battle. One wonders if any of the 5000 archers were mustered from Boxford. It is thought that the majority were recruited in north-west England. It is known, however, that Michael de la Pole, Second Earl of Suffolk, and his father took sixty archers to the battle. They lived at Wingfield Castle, a cross between a fortress and moated manor house in north Suffolk, but it is likely that their archers came from that locality.

The next bell was purchased in 1480 when the cloth trade was approaching its peak, and the other six were bought at infrequent intervals thereafter, with the last in 1799. They were continually taken down for repair at great expense. In 1702 there were thirty-six bell-ringers here, all of them illiterate, judging by their marks against payments in the parish accounts. Although they do not appear to have rung for normal services, they rang on every other possible occasion: victories, coronations, births and marriages. They were paid as much as twelve shillings (60p) a day as a group, provided the money was spent in the village. It is no wonder they were so keen! The last major bell restoration was in 1996 when the tower was strengthened.

THE PURITAN INFLUENCE

By 1595 the Puritan movement had taken a strong hold in East Anglia and Boxford was no exception. The Puritans were members of a religious reform movement that arose within the Church of England in the late sixteenth century. They believed that the Church of England was too similar to the Roman Catholic Church and should eliminate ceremonies and practices not rooted in the Bible. Puritans felt that they had a direct covenant with God to enact these reforms.

Our rector from 1563, William Bird, was a member of the Puritan organisation called the 'Classis of Dedham' which lasted from 1582 to 1589 when it was wound down by the 'malice of Satan' — the Bishop of London! The Classis was an informal and secret gathering of Puritan ministers in the latter days of Queen Elizabeth I, mostly from Essex and Suffolk. Much time in their regular Thursday meetings was taken up with their exposition of a Biblical text. Other business involved the placing of young ministers, just out of Cambridge or Oxford, in various parishes to spread their Puritan views.

In 1579 John Knewstub, a Classis member, became rector of Cockfield under the patronage of the Spring family, the wealthy clothiers of Lavenham. He was a famous Puritan and friend of Adam Winthrop of Groton, John Winthrop's father. He frequently preached at Boxford, and Cockfield became a centre of Puritan doctrine. In May 1582, an assembly of about sixty clergymen from Norfolk, Suffolk, and Cambridgeshire met in Cockfield Church to confer about the Prayer Book, clerical dress, and customs. Knewstub played a major role at the Hampton Court Conference in 1604, representing the Puritans. This was a discussion between King James I of England and representatives of the Church of England and the Puritans. Knewstub appeared as one of the four ministers deputed to oppose conformity. He took especial exception to the use of the sign of the cross in

John Winthrop (1587–1649), Lord of the Manor at Groton. He led the Puritan emigration to America and became the highly regarded first Governor of Massachusetts Bay Colony.

baptism and also to the surplice in Anglican worship, seeing it as a Catholic remnant.

Another Classis member was Henry Sandes (1549–1626) a 'lecturer' (preacher) at Boxford from about 1582 to 1624. Adam Winthrop and Henry Sandes were very close friends, and Sandes was buried close by him at Groton. In 1593 Thomas Chambers, our curate, was in trouble with the Bishop for not wearing the surplice in church. In 1606, Joseph Bird, Boxford rector and son of William, was accused of the same. These were some of the men who founded and governed the new grammar school from 1596 and it is clear that its teaching was intended to mould future generations in the same Puritan beliefs.

Puritanism remained strong in Boxford. John Winthrop (1587–1649), Lord of the Manor at Groton, was an important figure in the village until 1630. He became involved in the Massachusetts Bay Company in 1629 when anti-Puritan King Charles I began a crackdown on nonconformist religious thought in England. As a leading member, Winthrop was elected Governor of the Massachusetts Bay Colony in October 1629 and in April 1630 he led the main Puritan emigration of colonists on eleven ships to New England. He remained there until his death, serving eighteen terms as Governor. He was a highly respected political figure in the colony and a force of comparative moderation, but his attitude toward governance seems authoritarian to us today. He resisted all attempts to widen voting and other civil rights beyond a narrow class of religiously approved individuals, and he opposed unconstrained democracy, calling it 'the meanest and worst of all forms of government'. However, he is much revered to this day in the U.S.A. as the first governor, as those of us fortunate enough to go on one of the two exchanges in the last fifty years between Boxford and Boxford, Massachusetts, discovered when we toured the Massachusetts State House in Boston.

In 1643–4 St Mary's Church suffered the depredations of the Puritan William Dowsing and his assistants. William Dowsing was born in Laxfield, Suffolk and was made responsible for the seven eastern counties during early years of the English Civil War. In December

1643 he was appointed by the Earl of Manchester to carry out the Parliamentary Ordinance of 28 August 1643 which stated that 'all Monuments of Superstition and Idolatry should be removed and abolished', specifying: 'fixed altars, altar rails, chancel steps, crucifixes, crosses, images of the Virgin Mary and pictures of saints or superstitious inscriptions.' In May 1644 the scope of the Ordinance was widened to include representations of angels (a particular obsession of Dowsing), rood lofts, holy water stoups, and images in stone, wood and glass and on plate. Boxford church had amassed many such objects through bequests and donations from the wealth of the cloth trade. All of our silver ornaments, gilded and painted carvings, statues and sculptures and richly embroidered vestments were looted or destroyed by Dowsing's men, never to be seen again.

The Boxford clothmakers seem readily to have become Anglicans after the Reformation and then later Puritans. They were the wealthy and powerful leaders of the village and one wonders how they reacted to this pillaging of their church's wealth by the Puritan Dowsing. Between 1644 and 1646 Parliament removed clergymen with royalist sympathies, referred to in the political jargon of the time as 'scandalous ministers': 'Any minister who was non-resident, incompetent or idle, scandalous either in life or in doctrine, or in any way ill-affected to Parliament'. As the Civil War developed, two Suffolk Committees were empowered to hear evidence against any minister or schoolmaster who was 'scandalous' in either life or doctrine, or in any way 'malignant'. It would generally be the more Puritan parishioners who brought accusations to the Committees against village Anglicans or Catholics. This will have posed serious questions of allegiance here at parish level.

At least two of our own priests were investigated. One, Theodore Beale, curate in 1644, was accused of being a 'common alehouse haunter and a frequenter of pitchering and clubbing houses'. 'Pitchering' was demanding money for beer from a man seen out 'courting'! The meaning of courting is best left to the imagination, as are 'clubbing houses' which probably involved gambling at least. Another of his 'sins' was apparently bowing to the east end of the church—a Catholic practice in Anglican times. James Warwell, who became Rector in 1638, was said to approve of merrymaking and preached two sermons celebrating the restoration of the monarchy, thereby showing his royalist sympathies. He was therefore listed as one of the 'scandalous ministers' in 1646 following examination by the Suffolk Committee authorised by Parliament to root out such royalists. By 1649 he was nevertheless a governor of the grammar school and remained so until 1663. Puritanism was a very divisive force in the village for over a century.

BOXFORD RECTORIES

The parish church has had three rectories over time. The original parsonage (depicted overleaf) was on Stone Street Road where Parsonage Farm stands today. It must have been much bigger originally, with very many rooms, a longhouse, barn and gatehouse. The canal or moat there is a straight piece of water with slightly expanded ends on the east side of Parsonage Farm. It is possible that it was originally one arm of a rectangular moat around the parsonage house, but it was converted into an ornamental canal by the Revd John Warren, Rector of Boxford between 1683 and 1721. In 1723 Revd Thomas Warren, his son and successor, noted: 'On the East of [the parsonage house] buts upon a Green Walk bounded by a Canal of a great length & well stocked with fish; and made by late incumbent [his father], where before was nothing but a foul stinking ditch'. In 1735 Revd Thomas Warren refers to 'ye Green Walk adjoyning to the moat'. By 1827 much of the parsonage had been pulled down and Revd Thomas Thurlow built a new, much grander rectory with a Palladian interior, now called Boxford House. By the twentieth century the grounds of the rectory became important for village gatherings, recreation, fêtes, the village football ground and its tennis courts. This ceased during the Second World War when Bren gun carriers were parked there and it was used for training. By 1958 what would become Boxford House had become far too expensive for a rector to maintain, so the modern rectory was built on the glebeland, adjacent to what is now the new cemetery.

The old parsonage on Stone Street Road. This 1928 view of Parsonage Farm shows its moat and dovecote.

BOXFORD TOKENS

These were unofficial 'coins' in various alloys of copper and brass which were struck between 1648 and 1672 in many parts of England and semi-tolerated officially. During the English Civil War (1642–1651) the amount of officially available small change (farthing and halfpenny) was woefully inadequate. These denominations were vital to daily life in Boxford. Individual local traders therefore started issuing their own tokens after the death of Charles I on 30 January 1649. Under Oliver Cromwell during the Commonwealth period, 1649–1660, the problem grew and more were issued.

The following examples have been found of Boxford 'Commonwealth' tokens, with the dates and the names of the traders who issued them. They would have been used freely for trade throughout the village.

John Riddelsdale at the Sun 1667
  (presumably there was then a tavern of this name)

Daniel Bowtell in Boxford, Mercer 1648–1672
  (he dealt in cloth and other goods)

Mathew Teper in Groton 1664 (*illustrated below*)
  (the falcon depicted suggests he probably ran the Falcon Inn on the east side of Swan Street)

Thomas Goodall at the Falcon, Groton 1670
  (again at the Falcon in Swan Street)

Susanna King at the Swan 1664
(opposite the Falcon on the west side of Swan Street)

James Warwell Rector of Boxford
(probably issued by his son, a draper of Groton. The Warwells
were royalists, and the device of a fleur-de-lys and crown on the
token was probably intended to make known their allegiance.)

An official edict, issued in 1672 after the introduction of a proper
royal copper coinage, made the tokens illegal.

LIFE IN BOXFORD AFTER THE
RESTORATION OF THE MONARCHY

The Hearth Tax was introduced in England and Wales in 1662 to
provide a regular source of income for the newly restored monarch,
Charles II. Parliament had accepted that the King required an annual
income of £1.2 million to run the country, much of which came from
customs and excise. The Hearth Tax of 1674 shows there were 121
eligible households in Boxford, some of them in very crowded shared
tenements and almshouses. Each liable householder was to pay one
shilling (5p), twice a year, for each fire, hearth and stove in each dwel-
ling or house. Twenty nine households paid no tax at all.

By 1681 around 200 people out of a population of around 900 in
Boxford were regularly receiving poor relief from the vestry totalling
£105 per annum between them—a considerable sum. This illustrates
vividly how hard times had become with the decline of the cloth
trade. Money, clothing and food were distributed in the church
porch by the vestry. Money for the poor was obtained partially from
rent of land, houses, the windmill and shops, and the rest came from
bequests in wills. Bequests were often managed by small charities
and today these have been amalgamated in the United Boxford Charities Trust. Game (and poaching!) were an important supplement to
the diet of the poor. It is interesting therefore that in 1715, when
Henry Hart was fined for destroying game, ninety-two poor people
were paid a few pence from his fine. At the same time, to those killing
a fox or badger the churchwardens were paying up to three shillings
and sixpence (17½p): another considerable sum.

In 1684 a Mr Cooper of Boxford claimed that he employed over 200 poor people in woollen manufacturing. If this is true, and there were probably other employers too, the town's cloth industry was still hanging on, despite the marked decline. A 1697 Act of Parliament required our parish publicly to identify the poor with badges (total cost: £28) and list them according to how industrious they were and whether they attended church. The parish overseer was also responsible for burying the poor, and the parish provided drink for these funerals. Between 1650 and 1750 overseers of the poor 'bound-out' boys and girls as apprentices, and seventy-three indentures of apprenticeship survive. Nearly half relate to cloth and associated trades. In addition nineteen were sent to Colchester and nine to Sudbury. Some went into glovemaking and fellmongering (preparing skins), woolcombing and tailoring. Around this time there were several outbreaks of infectious diseases including smallpox. These particularly afflicted the poor and there was probably a 'pest house' somewhere here to isolate sufferers.

Around 1700 there was bear-baiting around a stake in the open space in front of the church at the junction of School Hill and Stone Street Road (called Bearstake Street in the parish record at that time). It was considered a great sporting and gambling event. This is surprising, as both bull-baiting and bear-baiting had supposedly been banned just after the Reformation. It seems that Boxford was doing its own thing again. The bear was cruelly chained to a stake by one hind leg or by the neck and worried by dogs. It was not fully outlawed by Act of Parliament until 1835.

There was once a processional path around the church which was used by the clergy, choir, gild officers, members and parishioners to walk in solemn progress at times of the great church festivals. In a rarely documented event in 1702, the women of Boxford linked hands around the church and steeple in celebration of the accession and coronation of Queen Anne: possibly an early flowering of a feminist sisterhood! The churchwardens paid for 'sack' (a fortified wine from Spain) for the women who surrounded the church in a dance known as 'clipping'. This is likely to have had pre-Christian origins and was probably thought to ward off evil. From the records, it does not appear to have been a regular event.

In the 1705 general election only thirty-nine people in Boxford were entitled to vote, out of an adult population of at least 500. It is known that there was a Whig majority here (this was not a secret ballot). This is further evidence of Boxford's free-thinking and independent view of the world. The Whigs believed in constitutional monarchy and were anti-Catholic. In this election the Sudbury constituency returned two MPs: Sir Gervase Elwes, First Baronet of Stoke by Clare, a Whig, and Philip Skippon, a Tory. Both parties were founded around rich politicians more than on popular votes and a few men controlled most of the voters.

The politics of England in 1705 were chaotic. The government was highly decentralized and there was unrest in the general population and mob violence during this election across the country. Over 100 years later Charles Dickens gave a riotous description of the Eatanswill borough election in *The Pickwick Papers*. It was based on his first-hand experience, as a *Morning Chronicle* reporter, of the notoriously corrupt practices at general elections in Sudbury and Kettering. This was first published in July 1836 and is one of the most famous literary representations of a British election. At the hustings there was intimidation of voters and the custom of 'treating' local residents with copious drink. He describes men 'fighting, swearing, drinking, and squabbling—all riotously excited, and all disgracing themselves'. One wonders what Boxford folk of 1705 thought of this very undemocratic process of electing their representative to parliament.

THE AGRICULTURAL REVOLUTION

The agricultural revolution brought an unprecedented increase in agricultural production as a result of increased productivity of land and labour between the late seventeenth and late nineteenth centuries. Agricultural output grew faster than the population over the century to 1770 and, thereafter, productivity here remained among the highest in the world. This revolution began in Norfolk with the four-course rotation, introducing turnips and clover between wheat and barley, in place of the fallow which had been necessary to allow the soil to recover. Turnips were grown in winter and are deep-rooted, allowing them to gather minerals unavailable to shallow-rooted cereal crops. Clover fixes nitrogen from the atmosphere which acts as a fertiliser. This permitted more intensive arable cultivation and provided fodder to support increased livestock numbers whose manure added further to soil fertility. There were improvements to the plough, and selective animal breeding led to much higher yields. Farm size increased, drainage improved and any remaining unenclosed land was enclosed for added efficiency. Improving transport led to better markets for farm produce, particularly with the coming of the railways from 1830.

It seems certain that a few wealthy Boxford landowners and farmers adopted and benefited from these major improvements, although most land here was already enclosed. The main cash crops were still wheat, barley and beans, and oats for the many horses. It is also certain, however, that these improvements initially did little or nothing for most of the inhabitants of Boxford who were agricultural labourers. Wages remained static and life remained hard.

Food shortages led to riots in nearby Sudbury in the second half of the eighteenth century as rural poverty became more severe. The mechanisation and factory organisation of spinning after 1764 meant that Boxford could not even sell spun yarn any more as the price collapsed. The pressure on the poor became acute and the need for workhouses to accommodate them more obvious. In 1722 an Act of Parliament recommended the amalgamation of parish workhouses to run in a single more efficient building. In 1780 the Cosford House of Industry opened at Semer, but it was another fifty years before Boxford joined, and closed its own small workhouse.

THE PARISH WORKHOUSE

The 1776 National Survey of Parish Workhouses shows that Boxford's existed before 1764 and housed thirty people. The first probably opened here around 1743 and cost £150. It should be noted that a small house with two rooms up and two down was expected to take thirty people! An agreement between Boxford and Groton led to the opening of one at Daisy Green in Groton. Early small workhouses had also existed at Hagmore Green and Stone Street.

We know that in 1764 the Boxford churchwardens appointed William Ide, a yeoman of Nayland, as overseer for three years. He was paid around £38 per annum. When John Bear took over in 1785 his salary was £46 per annum. These sound considerable sums for those days, but it was intended to cover the expenses of operating the workhouse as well as the salary. Almshouses, in the early days, were effectively workhouses. They offered food, shelter, clothing, and medical care to the poorest and most vulnerable, often in exchange for hard labour and loss of freedom. Women were expected to spin and children to work in the fields. They were the last resort for those who were poor, unemployed, disabled, or elderly. Residents often experienced maltreatment, destitution and inhumanity. By the 1820s the wealthy felt the poor rate levied on them was too much of a burden and action was demanded. The Edwardstone almshouses in Swan Street were built later in 1855 and were a charitable way of supporting the poor.

It is not known exactly where in Boxford were sited the two workhouses closed after the 1834 Act, but at least two were turned back into houses. The view was that poverty was the fault of the individual and the 1834 Act was designed to save money and set up a new poor-relief system to discourage destitution. In Victorian times 'paupers' were forced to live in these run-down houses in horrible cramped conditions, often with the whole family in one room, or split up on gender lines. By this time Boxford's paupers were sent to the Cosford House of Industry on the Hadleigh–Semer road, which had a separate 'pest house' for anyone infected. Boxford paid £155 towards this Union workhouse's running costs in 1856. To discourage dependency, these poorhouses were deliberately intended to provide harsher conditions than those of a poor agricultural labourer living with a large family in a very small rented or tied cottage. The Cosford Union Workhouse closed in 1923, but workhouses were only officially abolished in 1929 and some continued elsewhere into the 1930s.

8
FURTHER DECLINE
1800–1875

By 1800 the town had shrunk considerably in population and extent (but it was still referred to by local people as the 'town' as late as the early twentieth century). The industrial revolution largely passed Boxford by and its importance diminished further. In 1800 the stone bridge and the wooden bridge had gone, not for the first time, and the crossing had once again become a ford, showing the lack of funds to repair it. Wages in agriculture, the chief occupation, were pitiful. During and after the Napoleonic Wars with France (1803–1815) there were extreme food shortages and the poverty of our many agricultural workers increased still more. It is estimated that in 1811 Boxford had 135 inhabited houses occupied by 148 families and 702 people. This meant that, on average, there were around five people per family. There might well have been more had it not been for the very high level of infant mortality. Children were lucky to survive to their fifth birthday due to infectious disease. The average adult lifespan in England at this time was around forty years. This was probably also the case for rural labourers in Boxford, even with access to a regular supply of decent local food. Those in cities fared much worse with their food supply and sanitation problems.

Boxford took in French prisoners-of-war from a nearby 'parole town' during the Napoleonic Wars—possibly from Beccles, which was the nearest to here. There were up to 122,000 enemy sailors and soldiers held in captivity across Britain, but only the officers were allowed to go to live in parole towns. The non-ranking French soldiers were imprisoned, often on hulks, as it was feared that they would bring revolution and lower moral standards. Officers were given the

A wall-painting in a Boxford house by a French officer billeted here as a prisoner-of-war during the Napoleonic Wars, 1803–1815. It shows a woman on horseback.

opportunity to 'give their parole'—their word of honour, in writing, not to escape—and to live relatively normal lives in lodgings. Letters home had to be checked and approved and they were not permitted to walk or ride beyond the bounds of the parish. They were allowed to find local employment to help with their keep. Their arrival no doubt caused quite a stir amongst the more susceptible girls of Boxford! No wonder their parole included a curfew. One French officer used his time in Boxford to draw exceptionally good charcoal pictures on the walls of his place of residence. They are still there to this day.

In 1815 the Corn Laws were passed. These were tariffs and other trade restrictions on imported food and all grain ('corn'). They were designed to keep home grain prices high to increase profits for the landowners who still dominated political life. This had considerable political benefits at election time when most of the population did not have a vote, but the wealthy did. The Corn Laws effectively blocked the import of cheap grain, making it too expensive to import grain from abroad, even when food supplies at home were short, as they often were after a bad harvest. The effect on the poor of Boxford is not hard to imagine, significantly raising food prices and the cost of living.

As noted earlier, nonconformity was strong in this part of Suffolk and the increasing poverty must have strengthened it. In 1823 the Congregational chapel was built in Swan Street with a small burial ground. It cost £2000, with funds provided by Robert Ansell of Brantham Hall. He was a friend of an evangelical curate at Boxford and employed his time opening Sunday schools and cottages for preaching and prayers. He was especially concerned about 'the destitute condition of the villages around Hadleigh' and had a particular soft spot for Boxford. By 1884 it had a school, probably a Sunday school, with forty children. The chapel, by then the United Reformed church, finally closed in 1992 and was converted to a house.

The Great Reform Act of 1832, which widened the franchise, did nothing to quell the growing discontent. It gave the vote for the first time to small landowners, tenant farmers, shopkeepers, householders who paid a yearly rental of £10 or more, and some lodgers, but

This 1953 painting by Ann Tooth, who lived in Hendrick House, Swan Street, captures the old gaol and Broad Street at a moment in time.

explicitly barred women from voting. Opposition to the Corn Laws became more vocal nationally. In 1839 several Boxford bakers were baking bread from second-quality flour especially for the poor, having tendered for the job. Two fires were set in Boxford and one in Edwardstone in 1843 as part of the rural protests. This part of south-western Suffolk had the highest unemployment and the lowest wages in the county at this time. In 1845 and 1846, the first two years of Great Famine in Ireland, there was a disastrous fall in food supplied to England, but the main problem was not just scarcity but high prices caused by the tariffs. The labouring poor were beset by food shortages, poor housing and disease, which led to an early death and the resulting low life-expectancy. There was understandably much unrest amongst agricultural workers and their sympathisers, and feelings ran so high against farmers that cases of arson were a frequent occurrence. In one case heard at Boxford Court, a draper's apprentice from Polstead was sentenced to deportation to Australia for writing a letter to Sir Charles Rowley threatening to set fire to his property. Popular unrest eventually led to the Repeal of the Corn Laws in 1846, but conditions for the rural poor improved very little. As the century progressed, poverty meant that young men and whole families left the village to seek work in the expanding industrial areas of Lancashire and Yorkshire, which recruited for their textile mills across East Anglia.

In 1828 the village gaol was built in Broad Street. It is now a listed building and serves as a bus shelter. It was initially built by the parish in two sections for £100, as a lock-up and an engine house for the fire engine. One side had a 'water closet' over the river. It never housed William Corder, famous for the Red Barn murder at Polstead in 1827, and neither was he arraigned at the Fleece as some here like to believe. After arrest in London, Corder was held overnight at the George Inn in Colchester and then transferred, in the early hours of the following night, to the Cock Inn at Polstead, where the coroner's inquest on Maria Marten was to be held the following morning. He was taken straight from there to Bury St Edmunds for trial and execution. In 1848, one half of the lock-up was bought for £50 from the parish by the newly formed West Suffolk Police, Boxford Division, as their temporary prison. The Boxford police station was under construction in 1848 with a court house and cells. We do not know when the old gaol was last used for imprisonment, but until around 1940 it continued to house Boxford's manually operated fire engine.

In 1857 Boxford and Groton had agreed to buy a fire engine jointly, but there was much wrangling over it. In 1901 the Hadleigh fire chief made it clear that they would not be attending fires in Boxford any more. From then onwards, members of the Boxford Fire Brigade had their own horse-drawn manually pumped engine, brass helmets and appropriate clothing, and were very proud of their role. Fires are thirsty work and they seem to have been provided with plenty of beer at each fire they attended.

In Pigot & Cº's *Directory of Suffolk* for 1839, Boxford is described as a 'populous and respectable village . . . situated in a highly cultivated and fruitful valley between two brooks'. Quite what the many poverty-stricken inhabitants of Boxford would have thought of Pigot's glowing description is not known, but it was a good business advertisement for the village, which was its purpose. 'Letters from all parts arrive every morning at 8 *a.m.* and are despatched at a quarter past six'. No stagecoach is mentioned and one wonders how long it took for them to reach their destinations.

Pigot goes on, 'A considerable malting trade is carried on here; there is a manufactory for dressing leather with oil, and a silk mill has been lately established.' The silk factory employed six people. In 1868 it is recorded that three Mormon girls worked there. The tanning of skins took place in Boxford from Mediaeval times and continued well into the nineteenth century. Tanners are listed in the Muster Roll of 1522.

There is later evidence that the major tannery was sited at Goodlands Farm (now Goodlands Barn) to the west of Swan Street, divided at that time by the parish boundary between Boxford and Edwardstone. There was collar-making on this site before 1770 when it was bought by James Harbert, a leather-dresser and breeches-maker. In 1772 it was occupied by John Gotlieb Klopfer, a miller's son born in Germany. He had arrived in England in 1761 whilst in his early teens and he won several hundred pounds in a lottery. He developed the site as a tannery with a 'bark mill' where ground-up oak bark was soaked for days to extract the tannin. The tithe map shows that there was a large pond on the site to provide the water needed. The leather hides were then soaked in the liquor in a separate barn and then 'dressed' before sale. Deer hides and sheepskins were also dressed.

John Klopfer married an Edwardstone girl, Sarah Finnan, in 1775 and they had five children. His will shows he ran a prosperous business. By 1839 the business was in new ownership. The 1841 and 1851 censuses show a leather-dresser and seller, James Butler, and a 'currier' (someone who dresses leather), William Gardiner, living with John Sowman and family in Swan Street very close to the tannery. He was described as a master tanner employing two men. Later census returns suggest that tanning may have continued on the site until at least 1871.

Amongst the many trades linked to farming that continued for another century, Pigot in 1839 mentions seven maltsters. After the cloth industry declined, malting and brewing became major industries using the excellent local barley. However, the gunsmith and two female straw-hat makers listed do not appear in later years. Glovemaking and parchment-making from skins are also mentioned. It is thought that Huguenots, who fled persecution in the Low Countries for their religious beliefs in the sixteenth century, may have brought glovemaking to Boxford.

THE NATIONAL SCHOOL

In 1740 the children of tradesmen in Boxford were admitted to school for 3 d. a week, but it is not known which school this was or where it was. This is the first mention of a school for the children of ordinary villagers, but 3 d. (1¼p) a week per child would have been more than most could manage.

In 1839, after the sale of the two Boxford almshouses ('workhouses') and their contents, the Cosford Union agreed to spend the proceeds on building a schoolroom with a master and a mistress for fifty children aged five to fifteen. This had been encouraged by an Act of Parliament and the 1834 Poor Law meant the workhouses were no longer needed. The school was built on church glebeland that had been part of the churchyard. The foundation stone can be seen embedded in the oldest part of the present building. It was a National school which aimed to provide an elementary education in accordance with the teachings of the Church of England for the children of the poor. Until education became compulsory in 1878, it was probably funded by a mixture of subscriptions, trust funds, rates, government grant and children's contributions.

In 1849 a separate schoolroom for about forty children was provided for 'adults and children of the labouring, manufacturing and poorer classes in the village'. It used the grant of another piece of church glebeland for 'promoting the principles of the Established Church'. A master (£50 a year, exclusive of lodging) and mistress (£20) were appointed. It stood on the west side of Stone Street Road and it was later used as an infant school. Its site now lies under the A1071 bypass built in 1975. In 1884 there were eighty children at the infant school along Stone Street Road and seventy at the National School. The former was in use up to 1904 when the main school was significantly rebuilt to take over 200 children and taken over by the National Education Board.

THE KINGSBURY FAMILY

The Kingsbury family is one of several in Boxford whose records go back without a break to the sixteenth century. It was already established in Little Cornard in 1369, and it appears that two sons had moved to Boxford by 1540 when they undertook work on the church. This very old Boxford firm employed two hundred men and boys at its peak more than a century ago. Its work on the church continued right up to 1984 when the business ended. The Kingsbury families were responsible for much of the building work in Boxford for over four hundred years, occasionally not to their own benefit. In 1881 a new bridge was built against a quotation of £148 by Mr Kingsbury, but with a forfeit of ten shillings (50p) for every day after 1 September that the work was not completed. It seems as a result he lost £20 10*s.* on the deal.

In 1630 three Kingsbury brothers and their families set sail for America with John Winthrop on the fleet of eleven ships, carrying almost a thousand immigrants from England to America, that founded the Massachusetts Bay Colony. One of the family, Joseph Kingsbury, a carpenter, swapped his good land for marshland in 1637 so the first church at Dedham, Massachusetts could be built on solid ground. As a carpenter, no doubt he was instrumental in building this first wooden church. He and his family helped build this new town and its society.

Perhaps the best-known recent member of the family was Walter Bloss Kingsbury (1893–1976). He bought Peyton House maltings in Broad Street, converted it back to a family house and lived there until 1920. He then moved to Swan Street and developed Commerce House with its complex of buildings, a store and carpenter's workshop at the back. He lived next door at what is now Kingsbury House. Bloss served in the Royal Navy between 1914 and 1918, was a religious man and a firm taskmaster. He owned many properties in Boxford including, on Broad Street, the warehouse at №5 and Peachey's bakery. He was a leading figure in the village for many years as a magistrate, chairman of the Parish Council, and a founder and trustee of the village hall in the 1920s.

A Kingsbury's labourer in the 1920s was paid 8½*d.* (about 3½p) per hour and was sometimes expected to cycle to work in his own time as far as Bury or Colchester. A tradesman was then being paid one shilling (5p) an hour. As well as house building and repair, Kingsbury's made coffins and ran a chapel of rest with a register office upstairs. In the 1920s Commerce House contained a branch of Barclay's Bank, initially on three days each week, and later only on a Friday. This closed by the 1940s. In the late 1930s Kingsbury's still employed seventy men, with labourers being paid thirty-two to thirty-four shillings (£1.60 to £1.70) a week—still less than 5p an hour. This illustrates well the poverty of many villagers at that time. It would

During the Second World War these men played an important role in the village. Left to right: Supt Hurst, W. Bloss Kingsbury (builder), Freddy Wheeler (ran Government information film shows), William Sore (headmaster), Capt. Copley (U.S. Air Force Liaison Officer).

have taken one hour's work for a labourer to earn 9 *d*. (3¾p), the price of a loaf of bread in 1927. Today a basic white loaf costs at least £1 when the National Living Wage (the minimum) is £8.21 an hour—in working hours, a loaf today costs an eighth as much as it did in 1927.

Kingsbury's hundreds of years as a major village builder and employer sadly ended when it was liquidated in 1984. Examples of their fine work can still be seen all over the village.

BRICKS AND TILES

Making bricks and tiles probably began here by late Mediaeval times. Local bricks were certainly used in Boxford to build large chimneys in timber-framed houses in the late sixteenth century, and tiles began replacing thatch as a more effective, fire-proof roofing material.

The first written record shows that the family of Frederick Kingsbury (a separate branch of that of the above-mentioned Bloss Kingsbury) was making bricks at the time of White's Directory of 1844 and Kelly's of 1894. It is thought that he and his brother, William owned the brickworks from 1839 and the business was continued by his son and grandson (also Frederick, who lived at Wynne House in Swan Street) until 1896. The 'brickfields' were north-west of Cox Hill and accessed from there via the Driftway and from Ellis Street via Clubs Lane. On the 1884 Ordnance Survey map the brickworks, kiln and related buildings are clearly shown. It was only ever a small-scale industry for local use.

The works used the local 'brick-earth' deposits to mould and bake into bricks. These fine sandy, silty clays had a high chalk content and were perfect for brick-making, hence their geological name. They have an unusual origin, having been blown around as dust on the bare landscape just after the ice sheet melted. These fine silts and clays were then washed downslope and concentrated into pools by rain and meltwater. In this part of Boxford they lie just below the soil and are 12–15 m thick in places. The brick-earth was mixed with some charcoal, or later crushed coke, so that it would be self-burning in the kiln or 'clamp' once the fire was lit with faggots or coal. These bricks are known as hand-made 'stock' bricks and their colour varies from yellow to red with streaks from the carbon. They can still be seen in houses and walls all over the village. Unfortunately, as can be seen in some boundary walls, they weather and crumble over time, made worse by the doves which use them for grit!

The industry was highly weather-dependent and labour-intensive. Work was only possible between March and October and was all manual, from digging in the autumn, moulding and drying in spring to 'burning' in the kiln in late summer. As with farm labouring, the job was hard and temporary and often left workers unemployed, suffering poverty in the winter.

The demand for local bricks and tiles grew during the nineteenth century. The two Kingsbury families built several new houses including the police station, incorporating the court house. At this time many of our timber-framed houses had brick façades added in the fashion of the day, and more bricks were integrated into timber-framed houses under repair. Small cottages were built, for example in Cox Hill and along Stone Street Road past the cemetery, to house agricultural workers who usually had large families and could afford only the minimum rent. These cottages were often cramped and damp. The workers living in them were often unemployed or impoverished by being laid off in bad weather and in winter.

Coal for brickmaking only became relatively cheaply available after the railway came to Sudbury in 1849. Coke will have been available from the Sudbury gasworks after 1879, but before 1900 cheaper, better bricks would have started arriving by rail from Cambridgeshire. Demand for local bricks declined and the brickworks probably closed in 1896. They are marked as 'Old Brick Kiln' on the 1904 Ordnance Survey Map and Kingsbury is listed only as a builder by then. Incidentally there was almost certainly another brick and tile works at some time at the top of Brick Kiln Hill beyond Stone Street hamlet. There are signs of workings to the east of the road.

The census of 1841 gave Boxford a population of 1,121. It is not clear how this figure was compiled for a town that spread into parts of five parishes, but the actual figure for the whole settlement, rather than the parish, was certainly much higher. We know that the population

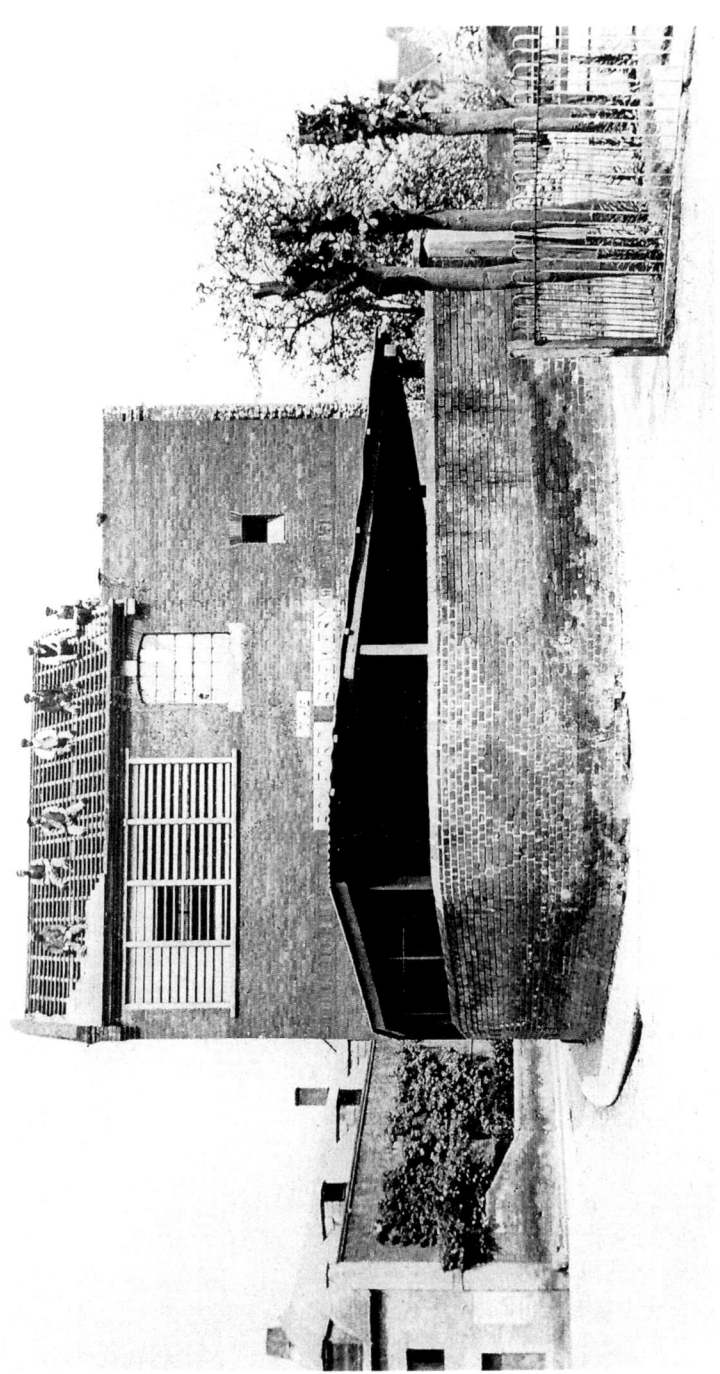

This large malthouse and brewery in the yard of the White Hart was taken down around 1916. Another maltings can be seen on the left, on the corner of Butchers Lane in front of Peyton House.

Tom Skinner, carrier, outside the Fleece in Broad Street, c.1911.

of Boxford reached a peak at this time and we can be certain that it never reached this level again until the 1970s. It is interesting that the 1851 census lists only 6% of the population as over the age of 65: an extreme contrast with today's longevity and age structure.

In 1845 'barrel' drains were placed under Swan Street, mainly to take storm water. Given that much of this street was then in Groton parish, Boxford and Groton agreed to share the cost. In 1839, counties were permitted to form and fund police forces for rural areas, and this was made compulsory in 1856. In 1848 the police station and court house was built at the foot of Sand Hill, still in Polstead then. In its heyday it had a superintendent and two constables and served a large area around. The magistrate's court dealt with petty sessions and pre-trial hearings until 1962. Sergeant George Beeton was said to be 'the last man standing' when the police station closed in 1969.

The excellent local barley led to twenty-two maltings being recorded in Boxford at various times, including a large one in the White Hart yard. This was only dismantled around 1916. Despite its poverty, Boxford at one time had eleven named public houses, and probably several alehouses or beerhouses as well. From the latter the lady of the house would sell home-made beer from her front room to farm workers trudging home. We must remember that farming was hard, thirsty work and the 'small beer' usually drunk in previous centuries was low in alcohol, cheap and safer than the water. It was really quite palatable and effective at delivering both the calories and fluids needed after a long day in the fields.

The Chequers in Church Street was in existence by 1495 and closed in the 1930s. Further up School Hill, in an old Tudor house on the right, was the Queen's Head (see page 101). In Swan Street were the White Horse (closed around 1904), the Saracen's Head, the Falcon and the Swan (closed 1994). In Broad Street there was the King's Head and, as today, the Fleece Hotel (a former coaching inn) and the White Hart. There was also the Compasses in Stone Street (closed 1989) and the Bakers' Arms at Whitestreet Green (closed 1957). The Plough Inn is mentioned in early eighteenth-century records, but its location is unknown.

In 1844 White's *History, Gazetteer and Directory of Suffolk* records; 'Boxford has several well-stocked shops, good inns and a number of malt kilns. It has a pleasure fair on Easter Monday, . . . and several corn mills.' This fair was abolished in 1872. The Directory lists twelve farmers, three blacksmiths, a wheelwright and five makers of boots and shoes. This would not have been a complete picture of the services here by any means, for this is paid-for advertising, but it does show that Boxford town was a major service centre for the surrounding area. It had a row of shops and services on both sides of Swan Street, along Broad Street to Ellis Street and up Church Street.

THE MORMONS IN BOXFORD

The Church of Jesus Christ of the Latter Day Saints (L.D.S.) is well known worldwide today, but it is surprising to find it here in Boxford in 1849, all the more because the Church had only been founded in the eastern U.S.A. in 1830, and the original Mormon pioneers only arrived at their final headquarters in the Salt Lake valley, Utah, in 1847. The 'Essex Conference of the L.D.S.' was formed as an offshoot of the London group and it was organised in Boxford by two British converts. The first Boxford Elder was a Scot, Ebenezer Gillies, a coachmaker aged thirty-one. His wife was from Durham. The Mormon chapel was made by converting the end of a house in Stone Street, now known as Old Chapel House. It seems it was led initially by five agricultural labourers and their wives, all living in Stone Street. It grew by twenty-seven members in nine months. In 1852 the Mormon Church in America made polygamy official practice, following an earlier supposed revelation from God. This must have been something of a shock for the Boxford Mormons. It certainly appears to have attracted a large number of male converts to the Church!

Between 1850 and 1858 there were seventy-nine baptisms of new converts, but by then this branch, like many others, had begun to decline. Actual membership and attendance in mid-1855 was little more than thirty-five. In 1853, aged twenty-one, Charles William Penrose became an elder at the Boxford Mormon Chapel. In 1861 he emigrated to Utah and 1921 he became First Counsellor of the First

Presidency of the church in Salt Lake City, a very senior role. He had more than one wife. In January 1854 David Paxman (a shoemaker) arrived as Mormon Elder in Boxford and moved on again in September 1855. His cousin, James, founded the Paxman engineering firm in Colchester and was the only family member to resist Mormonism. A brother of James emigrated and went on to have four wives. Mary Game, a Boxford convert from Little Waldingfield, was murdered by her husband when she planned to leave him, possibly to migrate to Utah.

Robert Dansie of Boxford and Charlotte Rudland of Newton joined the Boxford Mormon church shortly after their marriage at Newton on 8 April 1849. Disapproval of their new religion by their families and friends prompted them to sail for America in 1862 with their five children. There, near Omaha, Nebraska, they joined a church group consisting of forty-eight wagons and nearly 500 individuals. They started across the Great Plains on the long, harrowing journey to Salt Lake City. Sadly Charlotte and her eighth son Joseph died in childbirth passing through Wyoming. Her grave and monument remain there to this day in the wilds for all to see.

By 1868 the Mormon church in Boxford had shrunk to only five members, despite having absorbed completely the Mormon adherents from Ipswich and Colchester. Although energetic efforts were made to evangelise adjacent villages, these were often fruitless. It called for a very resilient convert to make the regular journey, doubtless on foot and in all weathers, to the small chapel in Stone Street. It was disbanded soon after 1868.

THE NAMING OF BOXFORD'S HAMLETS

It is interesting how much some local placenames of hamlets around Boxford have changed in unexpected ways since the mid-nineteenth century. When the first Ordnance Survey map of this area was surveyed in 1799, Tills Farm and another large one that then existed just to the south of it, called Salvetree Farm, were known collectively as Salvetree Green. Although never quite inside Boxford parish, this is interesting because, although the large farm of Salvetree was still there in 1939, there is no trace of it today. Bower House Tye was at that time called Mock Beggar Green. One can understand why this might have been changed! Calais Street was spelled Callis Street, meaning a rough track in Latin, and illustrates how modern spellings arise. Coddenham Hall was called Cadman Hall, and Sherbourne Street in Edwardstone, Shover Street. These last two could easily have been the mapmaker misunderstanding the Suffolk accent.

OCCUPATIONS IN BOXFORD FROM THE 1851 CENSUS

These are the occupations named, often with several individuals engaged in each:

Farming-related: farmer, labourer, shepherd, bailiff, gamekeeper, poulterer, pig dealer, dairymaid

Shops and inns: innkeeper, ostler, beerhouse keeper, baker, butcher, shop assistant, errand boy, post office keeper, letter carrier, ironmonger, druggist, fishmonger

Trades: leather-dresser (currier or tanner), tailor, straw bonnet-maker, staymaker (corsets), bricklayer, plumber, glazier, whitesmith (metal finisher)

Services: housemaid, nursemaid, cook, laundress, footman, housekeeper, chimney-sweep, hairdresser, charwoman, gardener, rat-catcher, groom, servant, coalman, roadman, house proprietor

Manufacturing: maltster, cooper, miller, shoemaker, cordwainer (shoemaker), harnessmaker, silk factory worker, brickmaker, glover, coachmaker, brewer, wheelwright, hoopmaker, wool-comber, basketmaker

Professional: cleric, doctor, schoolmistress, schoolmaster, dame school keeper, revenue officer, police constable

These occupations give an idea of the wide range of services the town of Boxford provided for its inhabitants and those of the surrounding villages and hamlets in 1851. It also reveals how self-sufficient it still was. The railway had only arrived at Sudbury the year before and had yet to have an impact. It was set to change this occupational structure greatly over the next half-century as local needs were increasingly supplied from far away rather than by local trades. It is interesting that the range of shops was quite limited in 1851 compared with the range of other services. This would change too. The Fire Order Book of the Yorkshire Insurance Company for Boxford, 1868–1911, lists forty-three different trades by name. This book was kept by Frith Dawson, the Swan Street postmaster until 1926. There is still a plaque on a house in Swan Street to show it was insured. This variety of trades and services shows why it was still called a 'town' by local people. It supplied almost all their needs, the rest being brought in by two Boxford-based carriers with a horse and wagon who made regular trips to Sudbury, Colchester and Ipswich.

The 1851 census shows that the average age in the village was 26½. At this time Stone Street hamlet alone had a population of 228. One cottage there housed twenty-one people, another housed twenty, and there were six more with eighteen or nineteen. The implications of this overcrowding for their health and well-being are not difficult to imagine.

OCCUPATIONS IN BOXFORD FROM WHITE'S HISTORY, GAZETTEER AND DIRECTORY OF SUFFOLK, 1855

Data for named individuals was collected by White's agents. They seem to have ignored the parish boundaries and, unlike the census, recorded the settlement as a whole. Unfortunately many occupations are not listed, particularly those of women and the poor. The following occupations, for example, were probably common: dressmakers, men and women 'in service' and agricultural labourers. None are recorded. Indeed it was meant to be a commercial list of important people by name and many will have paid for an entry. It cannot be regarded as anything more than a very incomplete record of Boxford in 1855:

> *Selling goods and services:* post office, newsagent, poulterer, watch/ clockmaker, fruiterer, druggist, three butchers, five grocers/ drapers, four shoemakers, three tailors and a stationer. We know that milk, eggs, butter, cheese and beer were sold from several front doors, but were not listed. Milk was ladled out from churns on a small horse-drawn cart and delivered around the village. No baker was listed but there must have been at least two.

Selling ale: five inns and taverns, three beerhouses

Trades: two saddlers, four builders including one brickmaker, three corn millers, three joiners, two maltsters, three blacksmiths, two painter/plumbers, a basketmaker, maker of gloves and breeches, and a cooper

Farmers: four farmers and four people living at named houses, presumably wealthy landowners

Professions: two 'surgeons' (local doctors), two schoolmistresses, one headmaster, a revenue officer, a police officer and a police superintendent

The arrival of the railway at Sudbury in 1849, and Hadleigh in 1847, brought new rapid prosperity to those places, but the immediate impact on Boxford was initially limited to faster delivery of newspapers and the post. Some goods such as coal and bricks would have eventually become much cheaper, but the railways did little to stimulate farming or industry here.

84

9
AGRICULTURAL RECESSION
AND A NEW BEGINNING
1875–1960

T HE major damage to farming was really felt about twenty-five years after the repeal of the Corn Laws, and as a result the population of Boxford declined even more rapidly after 1875. This was the beginning of a long agricultural recession which hit Boxford particularly hard, as it relied so heavily on farming.

Between 1873 and 1879 agriculture suffered from a series of wet summers that damaged grain crops. In 1875, 1877 and 1878, really bad harvests resulted. Cattle farmers were hit by foot-and-mouth disease, and sheep farmers by sheep liver rot. These poor harvests, however, masked a much greater long-term threat to British agriculture: the rapidly growing import of foodstuffs from abroad.

The development of cheaper, faster shipping (both sail and steam), the modernisation of agricultural machinery and the development of extensive railway networks in the U.S.A. allowed American farmers with much larger and more productive farms to export hard wheat to Britain at a price that greatly undercut Boxford farmers. The prairie farms of North America were able to export vast quantities of cheap grain, as were the peasant farms in the Russian Empire with simpler methods and cheaper serf labour.

Britain's dependence on imported grain during the 1830s was only 2%; during the 1860s it was 24%; but during the 1880s it was 45%. For wheat alone during the 1880s it was 65%. As an illustration of the effect of these cheap imports, the price of wheat in Britain declined from 56s. 0d. (£2.80) a quarter (28lbs) in 1867–71 to 27s. 3d. (£1.36) in 1894–98. By 1894–5 prices had reached their lowest level for 150 years at 22s. 10d. (£1.14). In twenty-five years the wheat Boxford farmers produced had lost well over half its value.

This was devastating for Boxford farmers and their labourers, as wheat was their chief source of income. Improvements in farm technology did little to help. They could not sell their produce and therefore did not have the money to pay wages that would have enabled the local poor to benefit from the lower imported food prices. The 1881 census showed a decline of 92,250 in agricultural labourers in England in the ten years since 1871, with an increase of 53,496 in urban labourers. The number of agricultural labourers overall in England decreased by one third between 1871 and 1901. Many of our farm workers migrated to the cities to find employment. It is little wonder that the population of Boxford was falling rapidly.

After 1896 cheap Canadian wheat was also imported in large quantities, prolonging the recession here. At the same time, large amounts of cheap corned beef in tins started to arrive for the first time from Argentina. The opening of the Suez Canal in 1869 and the development of refrigerator ships in about 1880 had opened the British market to cheap meat and wool from Australia and New Zealand. It hit the agricultural sector hard, and by 1900 half the meat eaten in Britain came from abroad.

Robert Ensor, the famous historian, wrote in the 1936 *Oxford History of England (1870–1914)* that 'after 1877 wages declined and farmers themselves sank into ever increasing embarrassments; bankruptcies, . . . auctions followed each other; the countryside lost its most respected figures'. 'For twenty years,' Ensor claimed, 'the only chance for any young or enterprising person in the countryside was to get out of it.' The decline of agriculture also led to a fall in rural rents, especially in areas with arable land. Consequently, landowners were suddenly no longer the richest class in the nation. The so-called 'Long' Depression was a worldwide economic recession that began in 1873 and ended around 1896 in most places, but not Boxford. Here it continued to depress farming and incomes until 1939.

WINDMILLS AND WATERMILLS

Over the centuries Boxford had several windmills and a watermill for corn grinding. In 1316 it had three watermills: one near Peyton manor, one just below Mascal's Farm ('Newton' mill, although it was in the parish of Boxford until 1974) and the watermill in the village centre where the Mill Surgery now stands. After 1300 windmills gradually replaced most of the watermills in Suffolk. A postmill in Boxford was blown down on 5 March 1604, resulting in one fatal and two serious casualties. The chief village corn mill was built just north of Boxford Lane around 1783. In 1841 it was a smockmill with four cloth spread sails. In 1861 these were changed to an unusual annular sail by Alfred Clubb, a miller from Colchester. After the modifications, Mr Gowler, who worked at the mill, said the sail was effective, turning in a light wind and driving three stones. Unfortunately the mill was blown down in a blizzard and great gale on 'Black Tuesday', 18 January 1881. It was rebuilt and restored with four conventional shuttered sails. It soon fell into disuse when large scale industrial milling took over. It was burnt down in 1901 and not rebuilt. Its cottages were demolished in 1960 and replaced by houses around 1972.

There were three other windmills in the parish in the nineteenth century. A postmill was located in Wash Lane, half-way down on the right from the Calais Street crossroads to Cherry Ground. It was on a high flat piece of land on the bend at the bottom of Mill Field. It certainly existed by 1783 and was recorded on the 1840 tithe map and 1885 Ordnance Survey map. It was demolished by 1910. Another mill was located on Sand Hill (the modern A1071) near the Hazels. It was built around 1824 and still existed in 1840, but had gone by 1885. Even less is known about the windmill south-south-west of Whitestreet Green, which was certainly there in the early nineteenth century. The presence of so many mills highlights the amount and importance of cereal growing to the village at this time.

The very fine watermill in the centre of the village on the site of today's Mill Surgery was burnt down in 1934. It may have stood there in some form since Mediaeval times and was thought to be on that site in 1491. It was owned and rented out by King's College,

This fine watermill with millpond was sadly burnt down in 1934 whilst Rowland King was still the miller.

Cambridge for several centuries. Cambridge colleges owned significant amounts of land and property in our area. In 1751 the watermill was rebuilt by George Mundford, who had just bought it from Thomas Green, miller of Wormingford. Somewhat surprisingly in 1798, given the normal level of the River Box today, B. Rattenby was recovered from the river and given artificial resuscitation. He may have been in the millpond, though it was not recorded as such. He survived and Mr Salter's resuscitation effort was reported to the Royal Humane Society, which awarded him its Bronze Medal. There were apparently numerous drownings in the river over time.

In 1822 the mill was used for glue-boiling and fellmongering as well as corn grinding. Fellmongering was the preparation of animal furs and skins ready for tanning. From 1896 to 1916, Stephen Scarfe was the miller at the watermill and also at the windmill in Boxford Lane. He was followed by H. C. Raynham and finally by Rowland King until 1934. By this time, the water power was supplemented by a steam engine, and even a small oil engine when needed.

When the watermill burned to the ground on the night of 21 August 1934, many in the village turned out to watch. The Boxford Fire Brigade of eight men with their manual engine were called as soon as the fire was discovered at 2.30 *a.m.* Jets of water were sprayed on adjacent buildings to stop the fire from spreading and Jack Tricker (Acting Captain) and Kenneth Stacey climbed up on the mill roof with buckets of water to try to put it out. Outhouses at the back of Swan Street and several house roofs caught light one hundred yards away as the wind was blowing strongly. They were put out using ladders and buckets of water by Jack Tricker and Bloss Kingsbury. The Sudbury Fire Brigade was called at 3 *a.m.* and arrived in twenty minutes, but by then the fire was at its height and the mill was largely burnt down by 6.30 *a.m.* Spontaneous combustion of flour near the grindstones was thought to be the cause and this was not unusual in corn mills. Apples baked on trees at the back of Swan Street, and chickens were roasted alive in their pens, according to newspaper reports.

After sudden heavy rain in May 2000,
Butchers Lane ran like a river for a short while.

FLOODING

Historically the worst recorded flood was on 18 September 1888, when water rushed through the village causing considerable damage to houses and the White Hart. In 1935 floods destroyed the remaining millpond and its retaining sluice gates and threatened the village centre. This was a great loss to the villagers as the millpond had been a major recreational centre, both for ice-skating in the winter and boating and swimming in the summer. It tells us something about the climate at the end of the nineteenth century that 'ice carnivals' held on the millpond were very popular. The best was in 1893 when there was a torchlight procession through the village, the river was lit with Chinese lanterns, and food, tea and music were provided.

In May 1924, after a big storm, water rushed down Butchers Lane one-and-a-half feet deep. In 1939 the village centre was flooded again. After a very snowy winter, the big thaw in March 1947 flooded the White Hart and Post Office Stores when the River Box over-flowed. In 1978 and again in 1988 a period of heavy rain led to flooding down Ash Street and Butchers Lane, threatening houses, but not entering them. More recently, flash floods through the village seem to be the result of short but intense rainfall in a major thunderstorm bringing more water down from Groton than the brooks and drains in Swan Street can cope with. This happened in 1992 when water, soil and stones ended up in Broad Street and the Post Office Stores.

A major flash flood on 13 May 2000, described locally as a 'cloud-burst', brought water lapping at the steps of houses in Ash Street beside the bridge and entered three of them. The water arrived in the village at 7 *p.m.* following an intense storm over Groton ninety minutes earlier. It was reported that the water in the brook rose five feet at one place in half an hour. In Ash Street the water was six inches deep and in Butchers Lane it flowed like a river. It escaped into Broad Street and flooded a 200-yard length of the street, lapping at the steps of the Fleece and finally escaping into the River Box. The White Hart was flooded and needed new carpets throughout. A 'river' almost one foot deep down Ash Street escaped partly through Riddelsdell's garage, over Ellis Street, down The Causeway and through

George Everett in retirement, tending his Butchers Lane garden.

gardens into the river. Fire crews were called from Sudbury, Nayland and Hadleigh to help with pumping out.

Since this flood, Babergh District Council and the Environment Agency have taken steps to increase the watercourses' capacity. There have been improvements to the culverts, channels and bridges at Fen Street, Ash Street and Ellis Street, and the Environment Agency has improved the River Box channel through to Stone Street hamlet. The building of the Station Field estate in 2016 required an underground attenuation system to slow drainage to the Holbrook Barn stream, since that has threatened Fen Street in recent years. Since all these various works were completed, there has, as yet, been no bank overflow anywhere in the village, even after very intense rainfall. The Weaver's Green plan off Sand Hill for another sixty-four houses proposes to replace that attenuation scheme with a much larger one. It remains to be seen whether these various works will be adequate to counter climate change and maintain the recent good record as regards flooding in the village.

THE LIFE OF A BOXFORD FARMWORKER, GEORGE EVERETT (1893–1984)

Peter Hardiman Scott (1920–1999) was the BBC's first political correspondent and a household name. He lived in Butchers Lane. In his book, *Many a Summer*, published in 1991, he tells the life story of his neighbour George Everett, much of it in George's own words. George was born at Bower House Tye, just over the 'border' in Polstead. His family moved down into Boxford in 1909 and he spent most of the rest of his life at №6 Butchers Lane. George was born on a snowy New Year's Eve 1893 in the middle one of the three attached cottages that still stand at the Tye close by the A1071. His father, Dick, walked in a foot of snow to Boxford to fetch the doctor to his birth. By the time he arrived home along the track, the doctor was already there, having come by horse and sleigh.

Betsy and Dick eventually had eight children and somehow they all got along in the two-up, two-down brick-floored cottage with no bathroom. The hand water pump was on the end wall outside and there was a privy over a hole nearby. Water had to be carried in for cooking and to fill the cauldron and wood-fired boiler for the large weekly linen wash. A tin bath was filled to bathe the whole family. The rooms were lit by simple oil lamps. Paraffin, coal and general goods were delivered by horse-drawn van by Robert Stiff of Kersey.

Dick Everett worked on the nearby farm, but there was no regular weekly wage because so much depended on the weather and the seasons. He generally earned about ten shillings (50p) a week, but could lose a whole day's pay on a wet day. It was probably a 'tied' cottage, in which case rent would have been minimal and considered part of the remuneration. It gave some security of tenure, but on balance was to the farmer's advantage. The Everetts often qualified for Parish Relief when earnings were low and this could be up to seven shillings and sixpence (37½p) a week. There was only ever enough to scrape through the week and life was hard. Betsy made all their clothes; jackets, trousers, shirts, dresses and aprons.

Needless to say the children were expected to work around the house and garden and to run errands. There were no books, games or pastimes in the house. There was too much else to do anyway. George's job was to collect the milk each morning in a can from farms at Kersey Upland, Hadleigh Heath or Polstead Heath. This meant rising at six and often collecting it for neighbours too. It earned him a copper or two which he gave to his mother. He would be home by 8 *a.m.* in time for breakfast of hot water with bread soaked in it and a knob of dripping for flavour. It was then a two mile walk to school at Polstead. George had other duties such as trimming the lamps, cleaning the boots, knives and forks and chopping kindling.

Once George reached ten or eleven, he found work after school on nearby farms, particularly at harvest time. This would earn him a shilling or two for his mother. Although wheat was by this time cut with a sail-reaper pulled by a horse, barley was still cut by scythe and sheaved by hand. There was therefore a huge demand for labour in late July and August when the school was on holiday. Betsy brewed beer in July to stop Dick getting too dry, as during harvest he worked from 6 *a.m.* until 9 *p.m.* The farmer was expected to provide beer all year round too. It was an important part of a farmworker's daily food and was very nourishing. The malt came from Kemball's in Broad Street, which by 1916 was the only malting left in Boxford. After the harvest the family were allowed to glean the fields, gathering up any ears left behind. This way they could get free grain, which made up to half a sack of coarse wholewheat flour to feed the family. George said there was no meat other than occasional rabbits, which were particularly easy to catch at harvest and made a good stew or pie.

Another source of income was stone-picking in the evenings around the time the crops were sown in March. The abundant flints in the boulder clay soils come to the surface every year when they are ploughed. They were removed manually for centuries, supposedly to improve yields. George, his siblings and his mother would collect them in a bag-like apron on their front. When full, the stones would be heaped up and the family would be paid by the bushel. Four evenings' family work would be enough to earn half-a-crown (12½p), a quarter of the father's weekly wage. The farmer would take the stones to the roadside where they were used to make up the cart track surface, all roads being unmetalled at that time. Roadmen would crack up the flints and a steam roller would roll them in twice with watering in between. The rest was left to the passage of the iron-rimmed wheels on the horse-drawn carts.

In those years there was still the traditional ceremony called 'Taking the Harvest'—the climax of the year. This was a bargaining at which the contract for getting the harvest in was agreed between the workers and the farmer. The head horseman was the Lord of the Harvest and he had to strike the bargain, often unwritten, with the farmer for say, six pounds per man for a month's work, or in less time if you could manage it. If it took longer, then you got no more money. The farmer also gave each worker a shilling each to bind them, and two bushels (112lbs or about 51kg) of malt for brewing at home. The Lord led the team of mowers and set the rhythm when they were scything the barley. The man next to him was known as the 'Lady'. The pagan fertility custom of placing a green bough on top of the last load of corn to leave the field still continued in George's youth.

Chapel figured strongly in George's early life. Initially he and his mother walked to the Baptist chapel at nearby Hadleigh Heath, but when he was older to the Methodist chapel at Polstead Heath. Once they moved down into Boxford in 1909, the family attended the Congregational chapel in Swan Street twice each Sunday. George would sit separately with his pals. As he put it, 'there was nowhere else to go, nothing else to do'. The chapel would be 'crammed' on Sunday morning and evening as it served nonconformists in Edwardstone and Groton, as well as Boxford.

George left school at Christmas 1906, a week before his fourteenth birthday. He immediately got a full-time job as a 'lad' on the farm as he and his family expected. He gave his weekly wage to his mother who saved up for a good pair of boots from Mr Gardner's hardware shop in Swan Street. George's hours were 6 *a.m.* to 5.30 *p.m.*, six days a week: sixty-nine hours. There was no legally required half-day off on a Saturday until 1926, and when he became a stockman he had to feed the animals twice on a Sunday as well. He would have to get up much earlier when he was asked to drive the sheep or pigs along the rough roads to Hadleigh Station on their way to market. In 1911, when he was eighteen, George demanded a 'man's' money (twelve or thirteen shillings a week) and got it. At that time the farmer would not pay the full amount until you could carry an eighteen-stone (114kg) sack of wheat across your shoulders.

In late 1914, during the early months of the war, not much news filtered through to the village, according to George. Occasionally a family lost a son or a father and the village shared the grief and mourning. Some farmers hid their horses because they were so valuable and they were so attached to them, but the Army came for them nevertheless. In May 1915, aged twenty-two, George went to Ipswich to sign up for the Suffolk Regiment. This was the furthest he had been from home in his life. His Army pay was seven shillings a week (35p) and he sent half of it to his mother. In 1916 he was sent to France and his skill with horses was put to good use at the Somme and Ypres. He survived, but by the time he was demobbed in February 1919 unemployment was rising rapidly and the cost of living was 125% higher than it had been before the war. Boxford had sadly lost thirty-eight men including George's brother Maurice. The village, according to George, was exhausted by years of conflict and inured to the shortages. Life was as hard as ever, as everyone still depended on agriculture in one way or another.

George returned to his old job on the farm as a 'day man'—a basic labourer—and then as horseman. The Corn Production Act of 1917 had guaranteed farmers a good fixed price and workers a wage of twenty-five shillings (£1.25) a week, but you could still lose money for wet days. In 1920 the standard wage was raised to £2 a week. The farmer could not afford to pay it and soon the Act was repealed and grain prices and wages fell dramatically. George lost his job, but he continued supporting his mum and dad in that cottage until their deaths. George moved from farm to farm for much of the rest of his life. It was in the late 1920s that George bought his first wireless, which his widowed mum much enjoyed: a Marconi, from Harold Peachey's shop in Broad Street. Tractors began appearing for ploughing on Boxford farms during the Second World War, but it was the late 1950s before all local farmers adopted mechanisation fully and abandoned their horses altogether.

George retired from farming aged sixty-five in 1958 with arthritic knees. He enjoyed his dahlias, for which he won awards at the village show. He also enjoyed a pint at the Fleece or White Hart until his death in May 1984, aged ninety-one.

THE FIRST WORLD WAR, 1914–1918

On 28 July 1914 Britain entered what was to become the Great War. The villagers would have had mixed emotions of apprehension and patriotism, not knowing what was to come. After all, the war would 'be over by Christmas'. In September 1914, when Kitchener appealed for 100,000 men 'for three years or the duration', young men from Boxford and everywhere else would have volunteered with some enthusiasm and because it was seen as their duty. For many it represented an opportunity for the first time to earn a much better reliable wage than the low, uncertain income of the agricultural labourer.

In Boxford volunteers were recruited either to the Suffolk or to the Essex Regiment, either in the village, in Sudbury or by visiting the depot in Ipswich. The Suffolk Regiment recruits then went to Bury St Edmunds barracks to be kitted out, and on to Felixstowe for training. The Essex recruits went to Warley Barracks, Brentwood for training. The local Territorial Reserves also responded by joining up. Many recruits, however, found their way into other regiments in other parts of the country. This must all have been both an adventure and a culture shock, for many local men had been no further than Ipswich until then.

Whenever there were soldiers in the village, the children at Boxford School were greatly distracted and attendance was down significantly. The headmaster at the time, Charles Porter, also complained that, having lost key staff to the war, the authorities were reluctant to find appropriate replacements, and academic standards slipped as a result. Farmers found it difficult without many of their men and horses, and women had to take their place.

The violence and horrors of that war are well-known and Boxford did not escape them. Of the 138 men from the village who served, the Roll of Honour in the church and the war memorial record that thirty-eight died, either overseas or later of their injuries. Some were maimed for life. The pain of bereavement in each family must have affected the whole village, for at that time everyone knew each other. This pain gradually gave way after the war to disenchantment with society as it had been before 1914, and particularly with its politicians and leaders. The rigid pre-war social divisions had broken down together with the traditional respect that maintained them.

The men who had served and survived often had a residue of comradeship and personal pride, but their horizons had been largely limited to a 'hole' or trench in muddy Flanders with sandbagged parapets and rusty barbed wire. The luck of having survived was often mixed with great sorrow for friends who had not, and many felt only relief when the war ended in November 1918. They returned home after that terrible war, put on civilian clothes again and looked to everyone as they did before 1914. But they had not come back the same men. By the end of the First World War the British Army had dealt with 80,000 cases of shell-shock.

FARMING, 1914–1939

In 1914 farmers suddenly lost their cheap labour and horses to the Western Front, making food production very difficult. Poverty was rife and the village continued to struggle throughout the war. Germany's submarine warfare resulted in massive losses of food imports to Britain. This meant food shortages became commonplace in Britain from 1915. The Government intervened and War Agriculture Executive Committees in each county were given the power to ensure higher productivity, direct the types of crops to be sown, and increase the amount of land under cultivation. Committees had considerable autonomy over their activities and the incentives they set. In addition, minimum prices were guaranteed for produce and minimum wages guaranteed for agricultural labourers. Rents for agricultural workers were also controlled.

The results were dramatic. The acreage of England and Wales under plough increased by 1.75 million acres by 1918 and productivity increased substantially. The Women's Land Army was created to bring urban women, usually educated, middle-class products of the Edwardian era, into the countryside in 'lighter' rural roles. In this war it did not prove very successful. Nor did it, by any means, solve the labour shortage on local farms. Significant mechanisation of our farms was still some way off. Although sugar and meat were rationed in January 1918, it never became necessary to ration bread.

Our farmers, and to some extent their workers, had briefly benefitted from the high grain prices, but in the 1920s these declined considerably. In 1921 the Agriculture Act, guaranteeing minimum wages and minimum farm prices, was repealed, and farm labourers wages fell abruptly by as much as 40%. The government was facing a potential £20 million subsidy bill for the agricultural sector, when other parts of the economy did not have such protection. The high food prices were unpopular with a predominantly urban electorate. Some farms went bankrupt and farm sales were commonplace. Previous restrictions on the import of Canadian grain were removed. These additional blows resulted in further falls in farm productivity, increased rural poverty, further emigration to towns and some land lying waste, even in fertile areas such as Suffolk. The Great Depression from 1931 onwards soon cancelled out some minor price improvements of the late 1920s. An agricultural worker's wage for a fifty-hour week in 1930 was thirty-one shillings (£1.55) on average, but less if it rained and they were laid off. That year a loaf cost 7 d. (3p).

In 1930s Suffolk the issue of payment of tithes caused much unrest, amongst small farmers in particular. A tithe (from 'tenth') was traditionally 10% of annual farm income, collected by church officials to support the parish church and priest. Originally they were paid in kind (grain, milk, wool), but after an 1836 Act of Parliament they had to be paid by every farmer in cash. Resentment about the tithe had been growing since the 1880s recession, particularly amongst non-Anglican farmers. Nonconformism was strong here from the Lollards onwards, and low crop prices and near-bankruptcy in the Great Depression led some farmers to make a stand and refuse to pay, most publicly at Wattisham, Elmsett and Wortham. In 1932 this refusal reached its peak and became known as the 'Tithe Wars'.

It is not known how involved Boxford farmers were in this unrest, but it would have been the subject of much debate here when, in 1932, Charles Westren, a farmer at Elmsett Hall, refused to pay his tithe to the church. If the farmer refused to pay, the courts could enforce seizures by bailiffs, who in many cases would take goods valued at far more than the unpaid tithes. In this case, goods seized from the Hall included furniture, a baby's bed and blankets, a herd of dairy cows, eight corn stacks and seed stacks valued in total at £1,200, for a tithe valued at only £385. This injustice made the national press and an outcry followed. Westren built the memorial stone outside Elmsett church to remind parishioners leaving it to this day of the injustice suffered. In 1936 the Tithe Act limited the tithes, but they were only finally abolished completely in 1977.

Agriculture remained the main employer until the late 1940s, when rapid mechanisation took place. Today it employs very few people here, but in the 1930s it was still the chief source of a very low income. It explains how dilapidated much of the housing had become by the 1930s. Many of the older timber-framed houses and shops were in a very poor state of repair and some were taken down altogether.

Agriculture did not fully recover from the depression until after the Second World War. The main crops here were still wheat, barley, beans and oats. Sugar beet was only introduced in the 1920s once motor vehicles were available to transport the raw beet to the sugar factory at Ipswich. Horse-powered reaper-binders and standalone threshing machines were now becoming more common. Steam traction engines became the typical source of power for these machines and they drew trailers on our farms until around 1950. The world economic collapse in the 1930s had inhibited purchases of farm equipment before the war. Consequently, farmers were forced to retain their older labour-intensive methods of cultivation and harvesting until the early 1950s.

THE STRANGE TALE OF THE OLD
TUDOR HOUSE ON SCHOOL HILL
(the site of 'The Paddocks' today)

The Joslin family lived in a small old Tudor house, formerly the Queen's Head, on this site during the late nineteenth century until 1911. Walter Joslin the elder (1835–1911) raised fourteen children with his wife Elizabeth in the original house, and agricultural workers lived in the old weavers' cottages behind. Walter Joslin, junior (1885–1977) was the fourteenth child, and uncle to Violet Tebboth. She came to live with the family in 1901, aged two, adding still more to the houseful.

When Walter died in 1911, a large, architecturally elaborate mock 'Old Tudor House' was constructed around the frame of the smaller existing real Tudor house. It was built very well by two Ipswich businessmen. A whole new wing with a great hall (40 ft by 10 ft), a vaulted ceiling and a minstrels' gallery was constructed with exposed studs, new traditional brick chimneys and many other adornments.

The First World War soon followed and the Edwardian optimism died. Around 1918 the house was taken apart piece-by-piece, labelled and stored in Ipswich. The intention was to ship it to the U.S.A. for reassembly, but this never happened. Eventually it was moved piece-by-piece to Billingshurst in Sussex, where it was reconstructed as Beke Hall by Captain Reginald Wentworth Alfred James Cosway. It was later, sadly, burnt down.

THE VILLAGE HALL

The village hall was opened in December 1926. It was built by Bloss Kingsbury and his men. Funds were raised from villagers through donations of a penny a brick. The shortfall of £660 was made up by Sir William Edwin Brunyate, K.C.M.G., J.P. (1867–1943) of the Old Grammar School. He was an important colonial administrator in Egypt before finally retiring to Boxford in 1924. He chaired the village hall committee and was an eccentric character in the village. He is reputed to have worn as many as three hats at a time, one inside the other, and raised all three to all the ladies, both rich and poor. Today, after excellent refurbishment, the village hall is a busy focus with many entertainments, Drama Group performances, meetings and physical exercise.

SOME STORIES ABOUT BOXFORD PEOPLE, 1920–1940
collected orally; veracity not assured!
Locations referred to may be found on the map overleaf.

Up to the end of the Second World War, Charlie Raynham and his son Dick ran the dairy at Brickhouse Farm (now Riverhall) on the south side of Ellis Street. Ten cows were kept in the meadow (now The Causeway) between the house and the river, and milk was also bought in from cows at the Spong in Groton. The milk was delivered around the village by horse and cart from churns. The horses knew just where to stop on their rounds and went out as far as Edwardstone and Groton. It was measured on the streets into family jugs at 3*d.* (1¼p) a pint. Leo Gant helped with the delivery and had a useful sideline in biting off puppies' tails! Apparently it used to be a common, if

The Old Tudor House on School Hill: most of what you can see is a large new mock-Tudor wing added to a small old Tudor house in 1913.

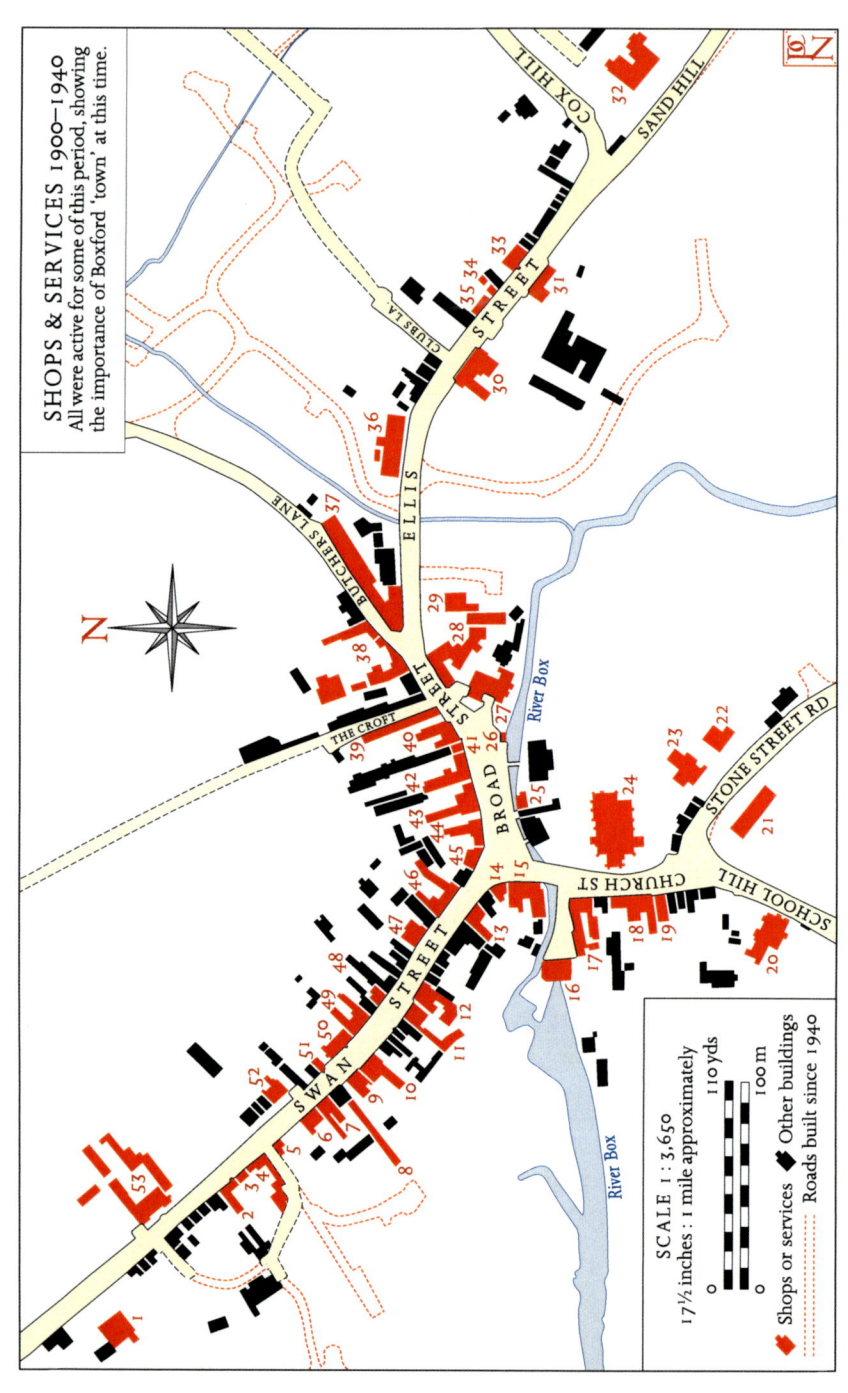

SHOPS & SERVICES 1900–1940
All were active for some of this period, showing
the importance of Boxford 'town' at this time.

SCALE 1 : 3,650
17½ inches : 1 mile approximately

◆ Shops or services   ◆ Other buildings
.... Roads built since 1940

KEY TO SHOPS AND SERVICES

(clockwise from top left)

SWAN STREET (*west side*)

1. Congregational Chapel
2. White Horse Inn
3. Charles Eley, fish & chips
4. Charles Godden, butcher & fruiterer
5. Frank Self, wheelwright
6. George Cady, baker
7. Webb & Sons, butcher
8. W. Bloss Kingsbury, builder & undertaker
9. Robert Sterry, toys & newspapers
10. Alfred Gardner, draper & grocer
11. Frank Stanley, butcher
12. The Swan public house
13. Annie Clarke, dressmaker, then sweets & tobacco ('Bottom Clarke's)
14. Edward Griggs, baker
15. William and Arthur Riddelsdell, later George Rickard, grocers; also post office from 1926

CHURCH STREET (*west side*)

16. Stephen Scarfe, corn miller (watermill)
17. Walter Bowers, carrier & bus
18. The Chequers Inn
19. Herbert and Raymond Stone, blacksmiths
20. Dr Alfred Thompson, physician & surgeon (before 1920s)

STONE STREET ROAD

21. Village Hall (opened 1926)
22. Infant School (formerly further down Stone Street Road)
23. Elementary (formerly National) School

CHURCH STREET (*east side*)

24. St Mary's church

BROAD STREET (*south side*)

25. W. Bloss Kingsbury, builder's workshop
26. Fire engine shed; earlier Boxford Gaol
27. White Hart Inn
28. John Moye, brewer & maltster

ELLIS STREET (*south side*)

29. Newton S. Rule, bus yard
30. Brickhouse Farm, dairy
31. Dr Dudley Beckit-Truman, physician & surgeon (from 1920s)

COX HILL

32. Police station & court house (superintendent and two constables)

ELLIS STREET (*north side*)

33. Charles Humphrey, poulterer; general store
34. Whymark Bros, motor engineers
35. Whymark Bros, general store
36. Riddelsdell Bros, motor engineers

BUTCHERS LANE

37. Charles Kemball, maltings

BROAD STREET (*north side*)

38. Charles Kemball, builder; timber; coffins; milk & butter
39. Riddelsdell Bros, cycle agents & motor engineers; later N. S. Rule's bus garage
40. Alfred Peachey, baker & newsagent
41. Fred Hynard, butcher
42. The Fleece Hotel
43. Aaron and Joseph Ribbans, Charles Barrell, Charles Stanley, Albert Cook, R. D. King, Chris Well, butchers
44. Eliza Turner, saddler; later Harold Peachey, wireless accessories

SWAN STREET (*east side*)

45. Walter Rugg, chemist & photographer; later Harry Grimwood, grocer
46. Thomas Skinner, carrier
47. Baker
48. Percy Mullocks, confectioner & general store; later David Coe, boot repairer
49. Charles and Frith Dawson, post office (until 1926), watchmaker, cycles, newspapers
50. Alfred Gardner, hardware
51. Elizabeth Clark, sweets & tobacco ('Top Clark's)
52. Walter Ribbans, pork butcher
53. Frederick Kingsbury, builder

barbaric practice in times gone by to dock tails in this way, both for appearance's sake, for gundogs, and to avoid injury later.

Gillian Harris was a very lively youngster and helped out on the farm until she was eleven, looking after the animals and driving the horses. She was very mischievous and Dick would 'punish' her in good spirit at various times by dangling her face down over a cowpat, tying her in a bran sack, hanging her from a beam, throwing her in the chaff pit or dunking her in the horse trough.

Charlie 'Plummy' Kemball, the maltster and builder, lived on the corner of Butchers Lane with a timber yard behind. He was a jovial soul with fat cheeks and a huge beard. The children looked forward every year to his turn as Father Christmas at the Sunday School. As well as producing and selling sawn timber, coffins and malt, his daughters, Eleanor and Emmy, sold milk, butter and eggs from the kitchen door at the back. Mr Munson used the malt to brew beer and sold it from his door close to the Croft.

The bakery at what is now the Old Bakery on Broad Street was taken over by Alf 'Puff' Peachey and his wife Maggie in 1924. He baked bread, cakes and pastries nightly and was particularly noted for his puff-pastry cream horns, hence his village nickname. As well as selling newspapers he specialised in 'celebration' cakes at Christmas and for weddings. This was a very busy and important business in those pre-supermarket days when bread was the staple food. He employed Claude Humphrey, Alec Smith, a girl in the shop, and two delivery boys at five shillings (25p) a week. After Alf died in 1942 the shop continued as a bakery until the 1960s, and even sold fish and chips for a while. Alf's son Graham also ran a bakery in Swan Street in the 1980s.

Our village had several butcher's shops in the first half of the twentieth century. I am puzzled why such a poor village would be buying so much meat. In the extensive hinterland to which these shops delivered, there was some wealth and food was relatively cheaper than it had been in Edwardian times. In the village itself a good solid meal of vegetables and potatoes with perhaps some meat was expected each day. A leg of lamb, for example, would have cost about one shilling (5p) a pound. An agricultural worker's wage for a fifty-hour week in 1905 was fifteen shillings (75p), so meat would not have been a daily event for all. On the other hand, potatoes, fruit and vegetables would have been largely home-grown and a stock pot would provide fairly healthy cheap meals. This way a small joint and some bones on Sunday could be made to last several days.

Five general butchers shops and a pork butcher (Ribbans) existed during this period. Meat was displayed in open or part-shuttered front windows in those days before refrigerators, and stored on ice at night. Three of them slaughtered animals on the premises: various butchers at Graham House on Broad Street, Webb on Swan Street (currently Leeder's) and Stanley on Swan Street. It was traditional, to meet the demands of the week, that they tended to slaughter on the same day (Tuesday). The blood was discharged through the drains to the River Box which ran red and smelled pretty badly in the summer.

What is currently the café in Broad Street was Turner's the saddler's. Then, in the 1930s, it was taken over by the latest 'must-have' technology — the wireless set. Alf's brother, Harold Peachey ran this. He initially put the sets together himself from kits and supplied the high-tension batteries and lead–acid accumulators so essential to running these early radios before the days of a mains supply. Harold delivered batteries and collected the accumulators for recharging over a wide area, until he sadly died at the early age of thirty-eight from tuberculosis.

Around 1926 the present Village Stores, №2 Swan Street, previously Rugg's the chemist's, was taken on by Daniel Grimwood (senior) and sold groceries and general household goods. He was known as 'Mousey' by the village children (though not to his face!) because he was always chewing a piece of cheese. This was his second shop because he already ran the grocer's in Stone Street. His son Harry with his wife Edith ('Diddy') ran the main shop in the village. When Daniel died in 1946 the next generation of the family took both shops on with their children until the mid 1980s. It became self-service in 1971. Ken King recounted the time in the 1930s when his gang discovered that by placing some lead in a hollowed-out cardboard coin they could get packets of 'Beech Nut' chewing gum out of the machine fixed outside the door. The gang was seen and reported, and Inspector Saunders and a sergeant visited the school to witness the resulting thrashing. The ringleader got twenty-one strokes and could not sit down for a week. Ken and the others each got five strokes. Ken believed he was saved from the worst effects by the thick pair of corduroy trousers he was wearing.

In the 1920s and '30s, №24 Swan Street was the workshop and shop of David Coe, a shoemaker and repairer from Groton. His wife sold draperies from the shop too. He was known to many as 'Pegleg' Coe because of his wooden leg, which he stuck straight out in front of him when making deliveries in his motorcycle and sidecar. Clearly nicknames were not given sensitively in those days. David used to help

Dick Elmer and Frith Dawson outside the old post office at 28–30 Swan Street

the boys in the village by putting a hobnail in their spinning tops for them. After he died, his pegleg was put to good use as a Brussels sprout dibber by Les 'Lardy' Gunn and was reputed still to be in use about fifteen years ago.

The village post office was located at Nos 28–30 Swan Street until 1926 and run by the Dawson family. Originally Charles Dawson was the postmaster and made watches and clocks there. His son Frith bought the post office and watch-mending and jewellery business from him in 1911, and his other son Frank 'Cuckoo' Dawson sold Raleigh cycles, paraffin and seeds from the other room. When a telegram arrived, Frith would summon the delivery boy, Vic Rice (senior), with a loud whistle from his work at Tom Skinner's bus depot at Ashley House. Frith and Frank had been very friendly with Eleanor and Emmy Kemball during the Edwardian period, and there are classic posed photographs of them in their Sunday best clothes, boating together on the millpond. Frith was remembered by Gillian Harris and other youngsters in the village for his very fast sledge. In snowy winters it was said to be possible to sledge from the top of Cox Hill right down into the village. Frith also rode a penny-farthing bicycle from London Bridge to Boxford for a bet—no mean feat!

Another bakery was located at №35 Swan Street ('Jacobs') until the 1930s. George Cady, the baker, was nicknamed 'Sue' after his wife, Susannah, who was known for the long hours she worked in the shop and bakery. She was always covered in flour and her hair and 'moustache' were white with it, so that she looked rather like Miss Havisham in Charles Dickens's *Great Expectations*. Her cottage loaves were renowned and farm workers' wives would pull the 'knob' off and fill them with butter, cheese and onion. One would be sufficient for both mid-morning ''levenses' and lunch in the fields with a screwtop bottle of cold tea, which had largely replaced ale by this time. The knob was left primarily to protect the interior and was rarely eaten because it got so dirty. Susannah would cook large joints for villagers in her oven at Christmas. George went round the village delivering bread from his handcart, and was well known in the pubs where he went to make up his books.

The wheelwright's shop of Frank Self and Dick Sargeant at 39 Swan Street.
Drawing by W. H. Caffyn, 1946

Boxford was well-served with sweetshops. The two best known were both in Swan Street: 'Top Clark's' at №34, Almond Cottage, and 'Bottom Clarke's' at №7, Lorne Cottage. №34 was called Tudor Stores and run by Tom Clark and his 'niece' Elizabeth Clark — at least that is how he described her. She was a 'lovely lady' and the shop was very popular with the children because it sold a very wide range of traditional sweets from tall jars in small quantities. It was still a sweetshop in 1957.

'Bottom Clarke's' was run by Annie Clarke, who was also a tailor. She was called 'Nitty' by the children, possibly because of an absent-minded habit of scratching her head. An ageing widow in the 1930s, she sold sweets, tobacco and Sunday newspapers. Her shop was a very dusty, untidy Aladdin's cave with lace curtains covering the sweets from eager hands. Ten toffees or aniseed balls cost 1*d.* — less than ½ p. Sunday sales were supposedly forbidden, but a knock on the front door after Sunday School would elicit a free sweet. The older boys clubbed together for a packet of Players cigarettes to share on a Sunday afternoon walk round Butchers Lane or the Wash.

Next door-but-one to 'Bottom Clarke's', at №3, lived Charlotte 'Aunt Dusty' Griggs. She carried on the family bakery after her husband and sons died in the First World War. She had already become the village midwife and nurse, almost certainly unqualified. She was usually sent for to deliver a baby and to 'lay out' a death. Charlotte was very much a Victorian lady who occasionally served tea on lace doilies to visitors in her perfectly presented drawing room.

A shop has stood on the site of №1 Swan Street, now Boxford Stores and Post Office, from time immemorial. It was probably a butcher's shambles in the late Middle Ages. William Riddelsdell was a grocer and draper there before 1880. Bales of cloth were ordered from London for local dressmakers and needlewomen. By 1922 Arthur 'Buck' Riddelsdell had taken over and it sold hardware, secondhand furniture, clothes, shoes, garden tools, fresh fruit and vegetables, cottons, haberdashery and tobacco. It was the most varied and largest shop in Boxford, with goods upstairs too. In 1926 it became the post office as well. The shop delivered far and wide, even out to Milden and Brent

The regulars outside the Bakers' Arms at Whitestreet Green in the 1920s, with Mrs Baker the landlady and Oatie Pattle in stovepipe hat.

Eleigh. Unwanted fruit was thrown in the River Box or in a pit up Cox Hill. It was 'reclaimed' by the village children, until one day Arthur injected the oranges with paraffin! They were much more careful after that.

There were at least thirty-seven retail outlets in Boxford between 1900 and the 1930s, although not all of them were there for the whole period.

The Bakers' Arms at Whitestreet Green must be mentioned here for this was its heyday. In the 1930s it was very popular on Sunday evenings when Billy Walker's dance band entertained inside and villagers came to sit and dance on the green in front. It was a popular Sunday evening walk up from Boxford. Regulars at the pub were the Pattle family. They were cattle and horse dealers of gypsy stock who lived together near the green. Their father William, from Norfolk, and his wife Caroline had eight children, the youngest of which were Daniel (born 1874), Oatie (1877) and Golden (1879). The family settled at Whitestreet Green in 1874, having previously roamed East Anglia, judging by the varied birthplaces of their first six children. The family were known to drive Irish ponies they had bought from Holyhead to Boxford on foot. There is a fine photograph of their father William at the Lavenham Horse Fair in 1896.

The three brothers were regulars at the pub. Golden lived to be one hundred and both his brothers into their nineties. It must have been very fine ale. Golden was almost mute and stone deaf and Oatie protected him from Daniel. Oatie was the cook. Daniel, the eldest, drove a horse-drawn Hackney carriage in London for a while. He was also stone deaf and very big, often riding bareback on private land around the village helping himself to nuts. When the Bakers' Arms was put up for sale in 1947 no-one bought it. Its trade had declined because of the shortage of beer during the war and the fact that local farmers had commandeered what beer there was for themselves by preventing anyone else from drinking there! It limped on until 1957 when it finally closed, much to the anger of the very loyal regulars. For a brief period an old shepherd's hut stood on the green selling beer as a protest, but it proved to be no substitute.

Milk delivery carts outside Rugg's the chemist, 2 Swan Street, c.1910

OCCUPATIONS IN BOXFORD FROM
KELLY'S DIRECTORY, 1925–6

It is likely that most of the information about individuals in this Directory was paid for by those wanting an entry. This may partly explain the small number of entries, but nevertheless by 1925 there were far fewer retail and trade outlets in Boxford than in 1855. Having said that, there were still at least seventeen shops compared with only four today, and between them they still catered for most needs, here and in the villages and hamlets nearby.

Selling goods and services: Post office & newsagent, Barclay's Bank (part-time), two confectioners, boot repairer, two cycle agents, two bakers, watchmaker, dressmaker, three grocers, fruiterer, two butchers and a tailor. The grocers sold other goods such as hardware and draperies. Cycle agents were vital renters and suppliers of daily transport for Kingsbury's workers to sites as far away as Colchester and Bury. Riddelsdell's were still listed as a cycle agent, not a garage.

Selling ale: Three inns or public houses, two beerhouses. There were actually six public houses at this time (The Swan, Fleece, White Hart, Chequers, Bakers' Arms and Compasses), which shows that not all paid for the publicity.

Trades: Two builders (Bloss Kingsbury and Charles Kemball), corn miller, wheelwright, thatcher, blacksmith, saddler and a carpenter. The traditional trades associated with farming were still much in evidence.

Farmers: Eleven listed. In all, ten other private residents paid for an entry.

Professions: One 'surgeon' (local doctor), one headmaster (teachers not mentioned), a police superintendent and two constables, a rector and Congregational minister.

In the 1931 census there were still seventeen shops in Boxford and all the major trades and services were still present.

W. H. CAFFYN

In 1930 a notable artist and illustrator, W. H. Caffyn (1870–1958), moved to Boxford. According to the 1947 Electoral Register he was

A view of the centre of Boxford painted in 1950 by the artist and illustrator W. H. Caffyn (1870–1958). This hangs in the village hall.

W. H. Caffyn in his studio at Hill House, Ellis Street in the late 1940s.

then living at Hill House in Ellis Street and one of his Constable-style landscape paintings from 1947 is preserved on the surface of the present bathroom wall. There are several paintings of his around the village including one (reproduced above) hanging in the village hall. He was most famous for his iconic posters produced for Bovril, Will's cigarettes and Bisto in the early years of the twentieth century. He also designed wartime posters including the very famous 'Come Along Boys — Enlist Today'.

TRANSPORT IN BOXFORD: THE STAGECOACH TO THE CAR

Before 1900 most people in Boxford walked everywhere and to their place of work. Most of what they needed was found in the village. Only the wealthy might own a horse, or a pony and trap or something even larger. Goods were brought in and taken out by carriers with a horse and wagon or cart. After the railway arrived in Sudbury in 1849, these carriers would have taken people to the station too. Prior to that, long distance travel by covered wagon and later by stagecoach, would have been slow, uncomfortable, dangerous and expensive. Nationally coaches gradually began to replace the clumsy covered carts after 1555. In 1620 John Winthrop reported the coachman being thrown from a coach in which he was travelling in Boxford. The horses bolted through the town until they came to a stop by the causeway next to the church. The coach was broken on the bottom and sides but John, his son, Mr Gurdon, coach owner, and another man were largely unharmed.

There is evidence that the Fleece was a coaching inn, but it is not known how, or at what times, it connected into the main Bury St Edmunds–Sudbury–London stagecoach route. Today you pass a now rare toll house on that route on your right at Sicklesmere on the way into Bury. This was a stop on the regular coach service that ran four times a day. Once known as Turnpike Gate, it was constructed in the early part of the nineteenth century by a Turnpike Trust, one of fourteen set up across Suffolk to maintain road surfaces.

After 1900 there were three carriers in Boxford who travelled regularly to Ipswich, Sudbury, Hadleigh and Colchester. Open waggons

Marshall Brown, carrier and landlord of the Fleece, outside Riddelsdell's in 1908.

with two horses were used for goods and passengers on these journeys. These were run by Thomas Skinner, Walter Bowers and Marshall Brown. The latter was landlord of the Fleece between 1912 and 1922 and he ran a very fine carriage-and-pair which gave comfort to passengers inside, with goods piled high on the roof. These carriers provided an essential service to the shops, trades and villagers alike in the days before the motor car and truck became commonplace.

After 1918 working men having to travel further afield could rent or hire-purchase a bicycle from Johnny Whymark in Ellis Street. He sold cycles on hire-purchase at one shilling (5p) a week for one year. These were fitted with carbide lamps front and back for Kingsbury's men to travel far and wide to work in the dark.

Roads before the First World War were usually unsuitable for motor traffic, and unsurfaced except for the old turnpikes. Between 1910 and 1939 considerable road-making was done by hand in and around Boxford and it provided employment for manual labourers at a difficult time. Many men returning from the war found employment of any sort scarce and seasonal, just as they had before the war.

From 1910 the motor bus and charabanc started to replace the waggons, but the earliest evidence we have is from a photo of Skinner's motor-bus stuck in a flood at Nayland on its way to Colchester from Boxford in 1919. The charabanc was a large open motor vehicle which could be used for goods or for trips to the seaside, with wooden seats added when necessary, making it an all purpose vehicle. Sometimes there was a detachable roof as well. For many this was the first way they visited the seaside from Boxford, always a source of great excitement, though not usually comfortable.

Tom Skinner delivered supplies to most Boxford shops and pubs (except those owned by Greene King) which he obtained from Grimwade's, the Ipswich wholesalers, and the Tollemache Brewery there. His small lorry was also used to pull the village fire engine by the 1920s. He was based at Ashley House in Swan Street.

His son, also Tom, known as 'Toggy', employed four drivers by the 1930s. Those fondly remembered are brothers Stan and Vic Rice (senior), Ben Rose and his son Tommy. Later drivers were Chase

Gunn and Claude Morgan. By the 1930s Skinner's ran bus services twice a week to Colchester, Hadleigh and Ipswich. His lorries carried grain to Hadleigh maltings and Ipswich docks. Skinner's bus business finished in 1936 when he sold it to the Eastern Counties Omnibus Company, which took over a lot of local bus services. Later he sold his site on Broad Street to Rule's, together with his corrugated-iron shed, which was moved from Ashley House to Broad Street. In 1940 Skinner moved his lorries to Calais Farm, now Mattock's garage in Calais Street. By now 'Old' Tom (Toggy) with son 'Young' Tom beside him would drive the carrier run twice a week between Ipswich and Sudbury. Until 1955 they carried parcels and Tolly barrels and bottles for the Fleece. From 1955 Dennis Skinner carried corn only, until the trade stopped altogether in about 1990.

After 1900 Walter Bowers ran a carrier's and funeral parlour with harness store next door, just over the bridge in Church Street. He was known as 'Larky' and ran wagons with two horses with a full load to Sudbury on market days and to Colchester on Saturdays. He reputedly brought back fried fish for resale and reheating, though what our own fish and chip shop owner thought of this, Charles ('Pickling') Eley of №43 Swan Street, is not known. The fish was re-sold cold by Whymark's in Ellis Street. If there was room on a Bowers wagon you could ride for a shilling.

For funerals Bowers used a hearse with two fine black horses, Old Yakun and Old Ronan, with red plumes on their heads. In the 1930s Bowers's son had a motor bus called 'Bluebell' which ran to Sudbury from outside the shop on Church Street.

Newton Rule lived at №20 Broad Street and set up his bus and lorry business soon after 1918. He used a long shed running along the west side of the Croft track. This shed, previously a malthouse, was probably Riddelsdell's garage up to early 1920s when they moved to their present site. The shed, demolished in 1948, stretched to the bowling green and contained petrol pumps. Buses would reverse into it via the Croft directly from Broad Street. They were convertible and carried coal and sugar beet locally, as well as people. They were scrubbed out, and covered seats were put in, for several Saturday cinema and market-day runs to Sudbury. A fourteen-seater delivered coal in the village on a Saturday morning and was cleaned and converted to a bus for the football team for the afternoon away game in Preston, Thorpe Morieux or an intense derby at Newton.

After purchasing Skinner's site in Broad Street in 1936, Newton Rule built a much larger business, but Rule's buses were still kept along the Croft until the late 1940s. During and after the Second World War this growing fleet of buses was washed each morning in Broad Street. Later, Rule's ran factory workers' buses to Sudbury and a wide range of other local services. The business on Broad Street (now Rules Yard) went to his son Archie, and then to Archie's son, Barrie, who was finally forced to close the extensive site in 2000. The competition for trade from the big 'nationals' had become intense, especially in holiday travel, and the closure of nearly all American airbases with which Rule's had contracts brought closure after more than eighty years.

It is thought that the Riddelsdell brothers opened their first 'garage' in the long shed next to the Croft in 1900. This would make it one of the first in the U.K. The brothers were the two sons of William Riddelsdell, the draper and grocer at what is now Boxford Stores. Originally it sold and serviced farm machinery, carts, bicycles and traction engines, but they soon saw the potential of the horseless carriage. The Revd Bonsey from Groton and his wife were early car enthusiasts and owned several which were serviced by the garage. The first private cars began appearing in Boxford by 1910. They were a very expensive but fashionable luxury for the wealthy. It was not until the 1950s, however, that privately owned cars became common in Boxford. The big surge in ownership really began in the 1960s, leading to individual mobility on a scale never possible before.

The Riddelsdell's garage we know today was purpose-built on the then allotments by the Groton brook in Ellis Street around 1920. It is surprising to discover that on the premises it manufactured 'Torpedo' motorcycles with two or three wheels. A soldered motorcycle petrol tank with the trademark stamp for Boxford is still in possession of the current owner, Howard Watts. Percy Riddelsdell owned the garage in the 1930s and lived at №6 Ellis Street next door. Later the garage was owned by Stan 'Jimson' Dyer and his brother, who returned from South Africa in 1919 after selling their goldmine there.

Further along Ellis Street was Whymark's garage and shop, which closed in 1998 and is now the site of №20, Whymark House. It was opened around 1920 by three brothers, Johnny, Bobby and Morri Whymark, to sell Elswick cycles, motorcycles, prams and gramophone records, and later petrol and car repairs. Whymark is a very old Boxford surname. Their parents Fred and Ann Whymark moved to Ancient House, Ellis Street from Lindsey with their large family in 1893. In total they had twelve sons and two daughters, though not all survived infancy. Nine sons were old enough to fight in the First World War. Remarkably only Walter, the eldest, failed to return, killed in action near Lille in 1918.

The history of this family reveals the individual enterprise that was necessary to secure employment by soldiers returning from the war. Johnny was in the Royal Flying Corps during the First World War, established the garage on his return and lived at Ancient House with his family. In the 1920s he was selling an Elswick cycle for £3 17s. 6d. (£3.88) and, with three-speed, £4 17s. 6d. (£4.88). Morri (Maurice) collected nutty slack (poor grade coal) from the railway yard in Sudbury on his three-wheeled B.S.A. mini-truck and sold it around the village. Bobby (Eric) sold Maurice's garden produce from two acres of land at the end of Clubs Lane, basic groceries and wet fish and cold fish and chips for reheating from a small shop built onto the left front of the garage. Another brother, Beetle (Ernest Albert) was known for his lack of enterprise compared with the other brothers. All were noted for arriving together at the Swan Inn at 9.55 p.m. and drinking only half a pint—the pub shut at 10 p.m. in those days.

Between 1929 and 1960 Corona Coaches of Acton ran a daily Boxford-to-London service which is fondly remembered by older village residents. Its heyday was the 1950s when it connected Kings Cross, Sudbury, Boxford, Hadleigh and Stowmarket. Several Corona coaches collected passengers at many villages and then transferred passengers to the necessary number of London coaches at Sudbury.

'Tornado' Smith trimming the claws of Briton the lioness at the Kursaal, Southend, in 1936.

The first coach left Stowmarket at 8.30 *a.m.* and arrived at Kings Cross at 12.50 *p.m.* This was hardly ideal for a day's shopping or a theatre visit, particularly as the journey took more than four hours and the coach returned to Boxford by around 10 *p.m.*

Kelly's Directory of 1937 shows little change in the number or type of shops, services and trades from that of 1925. Boxford still served a wide area. Two notable additions were Peachey the wireless dealer and Eley's fried fish shop. Riddelsdell's by now describes itself as a motor engineer's. This, when compared with the 1855 list above, illustrates just how little Boxford had changed as a retail and service centre in the eighty years up until the Second World War. Shoe repairs, milk, groceries, bread and cakes, newspapers and meat from our shops were delivered regularly within the village and the outlying hamlets. This continued into the 1950s.

'TORNADO' SMITH

George William 'Tornado' Smith is possibly Boxford's most famous son. He is certainly the most colourful. 'Tornado' Smith was born opposite the Saracen's Head, Newton in 1908. He was the first child of George Smith, publican of the White Hart, Boxford from 1921 to 1948. His mother Liz (*née* Baker) was from a Boxford family of thirteen children. George (senior) was also a thatcher, together with his brothers Chris and Marshall Smith of Stone Street. Before taking over the White Hart, George had run the Bakers' Arms at Whitestreet Green.

'Tornado' has been acknowledged by the British motorcycle industry as the first Englishman to perform the spectacular 'Wall of Death', a seemingly dangerous form of motorcycle entertainment which appears to defy the laws of gravity. It was particularly popular during the 1930s and was initially performed at holiday amusement centres such as the Kursaal at Southend by an American team. George (junior) first saw it in 1930 when driving a taxi to Southend. Immediately hooked, he then rode his motorcycle to Whitley Bay and there joined another American team as mechanic. He first rode for the team at Malmö in Sweden in September 1930 under the name

'Tornado', aged only twenty-two. On his return he became an instant star at Southend and nationally, extending the boundaries with new stunts, and later even using a car on the Wall.

'Tornado' met Doris Craven, who became 'Marjorie Dare' and later his wife, at Olympia when performing with the Bertram Mills Circus in 1931. She rode as well from December 1932 and they married in 1934. 'Tornado' soon had his own Wall and show and brought it to Boxford for the winter lay-over from 1935. He would usually provide a week of shows in the White Hart car park for the village. He was fêted as a hero and was a great self publicist using many stunts. As a celebrity, rather like a modern pop star, he featured regularly in the popular national newspapers. He was unique for a while in featuring a lioness, Briton, who sat in his sidecar during the act. When a cub in 1933 she rode on the handlebars. Local schoolboys remembered Briton being walked through the village on a lead! There is some doubt about how she met her end. Did she become aggressive and have to be put down with his revolver, or was she injured in a fall? The lioness was buried in the pub garden directly in front of the left hand front door. 'Tornado' continued riding until the 1960s and then in 1966 he mysteriously disappeared. He died in South Africa in 1971.

In the 1930s there was a regular annual visit from Bugg and Crighton's funfair to the White Hart yard. The 'Galloping Horses', organ and huge steam engine were much anticipated by the younger villagers. There was also a weekly cinema held in the village hall using portable equipment from Woodbridge, with a generator lorry parked outside as there was no mains electricity laid on at this stage.

THE SECOND WORLD WAR, 1939–1945
The First World War was supposed to be 'the war to end all wars' but unfortunately that was not to be. Only twenty-one years later, on 1 September 1939, Hitler invaded Poland and the Second World War began. Hitler's desire to see Europe dominated by the 'master race' and the need to defeat fascism made it inevitable, despite all attempts to avoid it. In this war ninety-one men and six women from Boxford served in the armed forces, and many more at home in an auxiliary

capacity or in the Land Army. In May 1940 many men, left behind because they were ineligible for military service, joined the Local Defence Volunteers. This became the Home Guard ('Dad's Army'), a well-drilled and effective team in Boxford by all accounts, which was obviously a cut above the fictional Walmington-on-Sea unit. Seven men did not return to Boxford from this war and the village remembers them on Remembrance Sunday each year, and the sacrifice that they made. Those who returned have now passed away, some very recently, having been characters in the village for many years. They are sadly missed.

In 1939–40, in the early days of the war, Boxford welcomed a number of evacuees from London. About ten years ago I met one of them making a return visit and she had very happy memories of her time here, staying at Boxford House. The room above the gateway to the old Chequers was used as an additional schoolroom as there was now insufficient space at the main school in Stone Street Road. In the past this room had been used as a 'reading room'. In the late nineteenth century a reading room was the usual way to provide working men with an alternative place to the pub for their leisure, to encourage self-improvement and discourage heavy drinking. Women would not have been expected to use it. Around the First World War it probably became available to women too. Books and newspapers were provided, most likely by donation. It is not known exactly when or for how long it functioned.

During the Second World War Italian prisoners-of-war were housed at Brookfield Farm, Cox Hill. Some of the buildings they lived in are still standing. They were allowed to go out when not working on the land or at the sugar beet factory in Ipswich. They probably considered themselves very lucky not to be fighting any longer. They used their skills to make things they thought the locals might buy, and, after Italy surrendered, they were allowed out into the village. It was possible to ask for a pair of slippers and the Italian would draw around the needy feet and deliver a pair of slippers the next week. One wonders what they were made from, given how little fabric there was to spare during the war.

HERE WE ARE TOGETHER
*The notebook of an American soldier in Britain
by Robert S. Arbib, published 1946 (extract)*

*Arbib writes of his time building airbases in Suffolk in 1942–1944, when he
was regularly sent from Wattisham and Debach to Sudbury, via Boxford.*

'More winding lanes, more little farmhouses for landmarks — a hundred turns, and then Boxford, the prettiest village on the road. One narrow winding street, two beautiful inns, an old church by the river, a winding hill, and our two girls at the big house. Of all the friendships made in England, the one with those two girls in the big house at Boxford was the strangest. It began almost the first day we made the trip — when we passed the house on the hill and saw, at an open upstairs window, two girls dressed in blue. They waved to us and smiled as we passed, and we waved back.

From that day on, every single morning, whether it was nine, ten, or eleven o'clock when we passed the house on the hill, the two girls would be at the window, and wave and smile. One was a thin, pale, blonde-haired girl — and one was dark-haired and wore glasses. Sometimes both would lean out and wave — sometimes just one. But someone was always there to wave the morning greeting. Those two girls were a baffling mystery. Was the big house a home, a school, or a hospital? Why did we never see anyone else around it? Why were the girls never downstairs, or in the garden, or out in front at the gate, where they could speak to us some morning as we passed? Were they nurses, or teachers, or housemaids, or daughters confined to an upstairs room?

For weeks and months our daily rendezvous was kept — and our greetings hardly varied from the original one. But one day we decided to break the mystery. On our way to Sudbury we would drop a note at the gate, and ask them to explain the secret of the big house on the hill. We stopped that day as we waved, and we showed them the note — and then placed it in an angle of the gate. They watched us from the upstairs casement, but they didn't say a word. And then we drove on.

Several days later, in the post came a letter, written in pencil, addressed to 'Bob and Earl'. It was from our girls in the window! It explained to us the mysteries of the big house. The house was the private residence of one old man—a Sir Somebody-or-other—and the two girls were upstairs maids. The reason they were always upstairs was that they lived in that room, and stayed there when their work did not call them elsewhere. One old housekeeper was the only other resident of the house. They asked where we went every morning at the same time, and they explained that they were not allowed to come outside to talk to us and, finally, that their names were Eva and Betty.

That ended the mystery of the two girls. We continued to wave to them as we passed, and for more than eight months they returned our greeting. We never found out which was Betty and which was Eva, and we never actually spoke to them. Our relationship had become so traditional and so casual that I doubt if we would have had much to say to them if we had suddenly found them down on the street in Boxford. We often wondered whether either of them had pretty legs, but in all the eight months we never saw more than heads and shoulders in the window, a white handkerchief, a white cloth, or perhaps a yellow scarf fluttering there, and always that warm smile of friendship.'

The mystery house was almost certainly the Old Grammar School on School Hill which was then occupied by Sir William Edwin Brunyate, K.C.M.G., J.P. The two girls are thought to have been Betty Gunn and Eva King.

A SNAPSHOT OF BOXFORD AT WAR

Evie Grimwood wrote nearly every day during the war to her 'intended', Percy Fletcher, who was in the army. He replied often and together they wrote more than 1000 letters. In one such, dated 5 March 1943, Evie described her day thus:

'I went to a Ministry of Information film show at the Village Hall and at about nine o'clock several parents came rushing into the hall and grabbed their children and said there was an air raid on. The operator stopped the film and we all cleared out of the hall. When we got outside, the whole village was brilliantly lit up by flares and we could hear bombs and gunfire which sounded very heavy. When I got home, Father (a Special Constable) shot off as apparently incendiary bombs had set fire to stacks at Peyton Hall. When he got home he said that on the way up they had put out crowds of incendiaries with dirt. They (the Germans) dropped some at the bottom

The last three Boxford veterans of the Second World War have lately passed away. Above: *Kenneth King, aged 17, at Brighton Army Training Camp in 1939.* Opposite, top: *Percy Fletcher standing next to a photo of his grandfather.* Opposite, below: *Cecil Hughes remembering Archibald Griggs at Authuile Military First World War Cemetery in France.*

6.1 George Fletcher 1852-1930 feeding his chickens at Turks Hall, Hagworm Green. Percy Fletcher's Grandfather.

of Stone Street but luckily missed the thatched cottages. As usual there was a 'muck up' over the fire engine as they had to wait an hour for it to come from Hadleigh and I don't think it arrived until about an hour after the bombs fell. There were three stacks on fire, two of straw and one of clover. It was the worst night we have had here.'

In a later letter, Evie goes on to say that they were still finding bombs four days later and that the Home Guard had the job of searching them out. Apparently little damage was done. One might wonder why so many bombs were dropped on this rural area. It is likely they were attacking the 'dummy' airfield set up as a decoy between Brick Kiln Hill and Stoke Road. In a much later letter on 18 September 1944 Evie mentions hundreds of gliders in the sky over Boxford being towed by two-engined and four-engined bombers. This will have been Operation Market Garden—the attempted invasion of the Netherlands, although this attack by the British First Airborne Division on Arnhem bridge ultimately failed. Evie said, 'I think we all offered up a silent prayer for those chaps when we saw the gliders'.

VICTORY IN EUROPE, 8 MAY 1945

Evie Grimwood described this as an evening of whoopee in Boxford, with the Fleece and the Swan overflowing, people in fancy dress, and an unofficial bonfire in the street. There was much drinking, which ended up with 'several of the usual chaps fighting until they got black eyes'.

On 10 May 1945 Evie Grimwood wrote again to her husband-to-be, Percy Fletcher, to let him know about events in the village the previous evening (9th) to celebrate victory in Europe. She wrote:

'At about nine o'clock Vera and I went round to the Hall to the dance. Everyone was looking very gay in their red, white and blue. I wore my blue frock with red sash and white buttonhole.... At about 10.45 *p.m.* they came into the Hall and announced that the bonfire was about to be lit and Hitler cremated. Thus we all put on our coats and paraded off down the street. My dancing partner—a Yank—insisted on escorting me and I thought to myself that this will give them something to talk about.... All day they had an effigy

The 1947 emergency 'pre-fabs' being demolished and replaced by flats at the entrance to Homefield in 1973.

Littlebury Cottages, in front of the church in Stone Street Road, were unfit for habitation by 1920 and were demolished. The blacksmith's forge in Church Street (left) is in poor condition too.

of Hitler hung up by the White Hart. Q. Gant made a coffin complete with handles and once the fire was lit he (Hitler) was put in the coffin and they bore him through the street amid much cheering. He was then laid in state and whosoever liked could go and give him a kick or spit at him. Then it was left to the women to put the coffin on the fire. Of course 'yours truly' had to have a go at that. It was a marvellous fire . . . but dad had got his hose ready. Hilda [Rule] played her accordion, Bill the drums and we had dancing around the fire. The fire died down about one o'clock and after "Auld Lang Syne" and "God save the King", everyone began to disperse and so we packed off to bed.'

HOUSING NEEDS AND SUPPLY

Between 1885 and 1950, with poverty and a declining population, there was little money for new housing development. Any new building was largely piecemeal and one or two houses only, even in the 1930s. Much of Boxford's housing stock was in very poor condition by the 1920s and 1930s. There was a desperate need to re-house many of the working people in the village, to keep labourers here on the land and provide homes for the returning soldiers. An Act of Parliament in 1919 required local councils to build some 'council houses'. As a consequence the semi-detached houses in Boxford Lane were built by Cosford Rural District Council in 1923. Building on the Homefield to the east of Swan Street in 1937–8 (Nos 1–6) by Cosford Rural District Council began following the 1935 Housing Act. The first houses on Swan Street were called Bonsey Terrace after Councillor Revd William Henry Bonsey of Groton, on land that had in 1934 become part of Boxford parish for the first time. In 1947 eight temporary 'pre-fabs' were built, as demand for housing after the war was acute. These were replaced in 1973 by the flats at the entrance to Homefield. The rest of Homefield was built between 1950 and 1953.

Some of the old timber-framed houses and worker's cottages from earlier centuries were decaying, neglected and unfit for habitation in the period 1900–1960, and some had to be taken down. Ancient House, the fifteenth-century clothier's house in Ellis Street described earlier, was one such. It was due to be demolished but was one of many to be repaired and renovated in the 1970s.

When it was for sale in 1986 (above), Ancient House in Ellis Street, built in 1485, was dilapidated. It was saved and renovated, and looks like this today (below).

WATER SUPPLY AND WASTE DISPOSAL

In the 1920s and 1930s water was still collected in buckets from the many communal cast-iron hand pumps around the village, or even from the river and ponds. Many hand-pumps drew water from shallow wells at risk of serious pollution. In 1936 Cosford Rural District Council obtained a grant to provide mains water to the village. The waterworks was built by Kingsbury's at the top of Cox Hill in the grounds of Cox Hill House, using a 261-feet-deep borehole into the chalk below, with the capacity to supply 51,840 gallons daily. The pump-house, built of attractive Fletton brick, still stands. The water was pumped to a tower that held three days' supply and was, in due course, piped throughout the village. This ended the task of fetching it several times a day and enabled ordinary people to have running water, modern baths and flush toilets. Although a house connection up to the edge of each property was free, many could not afford further installation but were pleased to use the new standpipes placed at frequent intervals along the streets. A fine example of a Victorian-style cast-iron 'tap' fed by gravity from the new water tower still stands at the junction of Broad Street and Butchers Lane. It was the late 1940s before all residents could afford connection to the main.

Many people still had an outdoor bucket toilet and 'night soil' was collected nightly from these until the late 1950s by the horse-drawn, rubber-tyred 'honey cart' which had a specially designed tank. The contents were disposed of in a pit. By this time many houses in the village had connected foul water pipes from flush toilets to a septic tank, or even to the storm drains under the streets which discharged directly into the River Box. A dedicated sewage system was begun in 1953 by Cosford Rural District Council which involved digging up the main streets and laying pipes. Houses were connected and all foul water was switched to this system from the storm drains in Swan Street, Ellis Street and Church Street in 1961. From a node near the White Hart this system uses gravity down the valley to Stone Street hamlet, from where it is pumped up to the sewage treatment plant above the ford at Wash Lane. It did not serve outlying parts of the village including Whitestreet Green until the late 1960s.

ELECTRICITY SUPPLY

Distribution of alternating current electricity from the generator at Sudbury reached Boxford in 1935, and the company offered to provide three lights and one five-amp socket free to each household. It was some years before everyone could afford to have electricity throughout the house and for heating, as we have today.

HEALTH CARE

1693 is the earliest date at which a 'surgeon' or doctor is mentioned in the parish accounts. In 1722 the Parish Meeting decreed that midwives should be paid no more than one shilling (5p) for delivering a baby. In 1738 Mr Thomas Alston was registered by the Bishop to practise surgery and was paid £6 by the parish to attend to all those who were unable to support themselves. He lived at, and practised from, Hendrick House in Swan Street. He was succeeded by James Tuson and several other doctors, all of whom lived at, and practised in a surgery at the rear of, Hendrick House.

From 1894 to 1917 Dr Alfred Thompson lived in and had his surgery at The Knollgate on School Hill. He also extracted teeth, with the patient sitting between the shafts of a pony trap and gripping hard! Dr Everitt from Hadleigh held a surgery at Kemball House in Broad Street twice a week in the 1920s and '30s. He was a tough ex-army doctor who, it is said, 'attracted the rich', whilst the 'poor' went to Dr Dudley Beckit-Truman at Greenbank in Ellis Street until the 1940s. His practice was then taken over by Dr O. C. Barnes who used a room at the White Hart. After 1945 this surgery was moved to a spare kitchen at the Rectory (now Boxford House) by Dr Jack Debenham. Three years later the Labour Party brought in the National Health Service which provided free and equal treatment for all.

Today's well-equipped Mill Surgery on the site of the old watermill was first opened in the 1950s by Dr Debenham and in the 1990s there was also a surgery behind Peyton House in Ash Street run by his son, Dr Michael Debenham. In 2020 the village also has a privately owned medical centre and two therapy centres.

Gerry Hazell with harrow and Suffolk Punches after a lifetime's work for all three. Gerry, in retirement, when not with his beloved horses, was to be found most days in the White Hart.

Long-time resident Derrick 'Von' Whymark, still working in 1999.

An oil painting by Elizabeth Gardiner of the 'green' at Hagmore Green with Derrick and Eileen Whymark's cottage.

An early combine harvester drawn by a Bren gun carrier driven by Vic Rice (jnr) in 1951.

10
1960 TO THE PRESENT DAY

CHANGES TO FARMING AND LOCAL OCCUPATIONS

In the early 1950s the tractor rapidly replaced the horse and the related oat-growing. With the gradual introduction of the combine harvester and a wide variety of specialist machines, a much smaller number of Boxford people were required to work the land, and wages improved for those that did. Nationally between 1949 and the early 1960s the number of agricultural workers (excluding farmers) more than halved in twelve years. One reason for this dramatic decline was the introduction of the combine harvester. The 1971 *Survey of Agriculture in Suffolk* by P. J. O. Trist recorded 118 combine harvesters across Suffolk in 1946, 2080 in 1956 and 2940 in 1962. By 1971 this had levelled out at around 3000, an average of six per parish!

By 2010 less than one fifth of the number of people employed in 1949 were working on the land. Fortunately for the many agricultural workers in Boxford, the country became rapidly more prosperous after 1960, and with prosperity came new employment and better paid opportunities locally and in nearby towns, pushing up local wages. Despite this reduction in farm labour, science and new technology in farming led to a considerable increase in farm productivity of 80% between 1953 and 1983. This new wealth also contributed to the growing prosperity of Boxford itself.

These changes had their downside. The availability of transport and the growth of supermarkets, jobs and services in Sudbury, Hadleigh and beyond meant that people no longer relied on the village for their everyday needs. Shopping by bus or car became the norm.

Boxford Stores and post office under threat of closure in 2012.

This was the death-knell for many of our remaining shops and services which had been in decline since the 1930s. Lifestyles changed rapidly and a much larger range and choice of goods was expected than our shops could ever provide. By 1994 only two of the many pubs remained. As I write in 2020, one of those, the Fleece, has been looking for a new landlord for some time. We are fortunate still to have a butcher (Leeder's), a Post Office and provisions shop (Boxford Stores), a small supermarket (The Village Stores), a wine shop and café and a hairdresser's. The car now dominates the village in so many ways and two of the three original garages remain to support them. 'Use it or lose it' is the maxim if we are to save those shops and services that remain.

THE INFLUX OF NEW INHABITANTS

With growing post-war prosperity, an influx of retirees and professional people from outside arrived to live in Boxford, commuting to surrounding towns to work in shops and offices. This was possible as wages were rising rapidly. Increasingly, after 1955, working people could even afford to buy a car. Incomers and the motor vehicle brought the rebirth of Boxford and a new prosperity, but also the threat to our village infrastructure we see today from traffic conflict, congestion and parking. The Conservation Area was established in 1973 to protect the ancient heart of the village, and between 1989 and 1992 the many overhead cables in it were buried.

The affordability of the motor car had encouraged the influx of new inhabitants, particularly between 1960 and 1980. This attractive Mediaeval village nestling in its valley had immediate appeal for those wanting to move to the country from the cities and London. The existing housing stock was very run down but cheap to buy. It was mainly these incomers who began the renovation of the old dilapidated houses. The car made commuting possible for those not yet of retirement age, not only to nearby towns but to Colchester, where they could use the by now electrified railway to London.

These 'outsiders', with their new ideas of how things should be done and their relative wealth, were not always popular with the 'old'

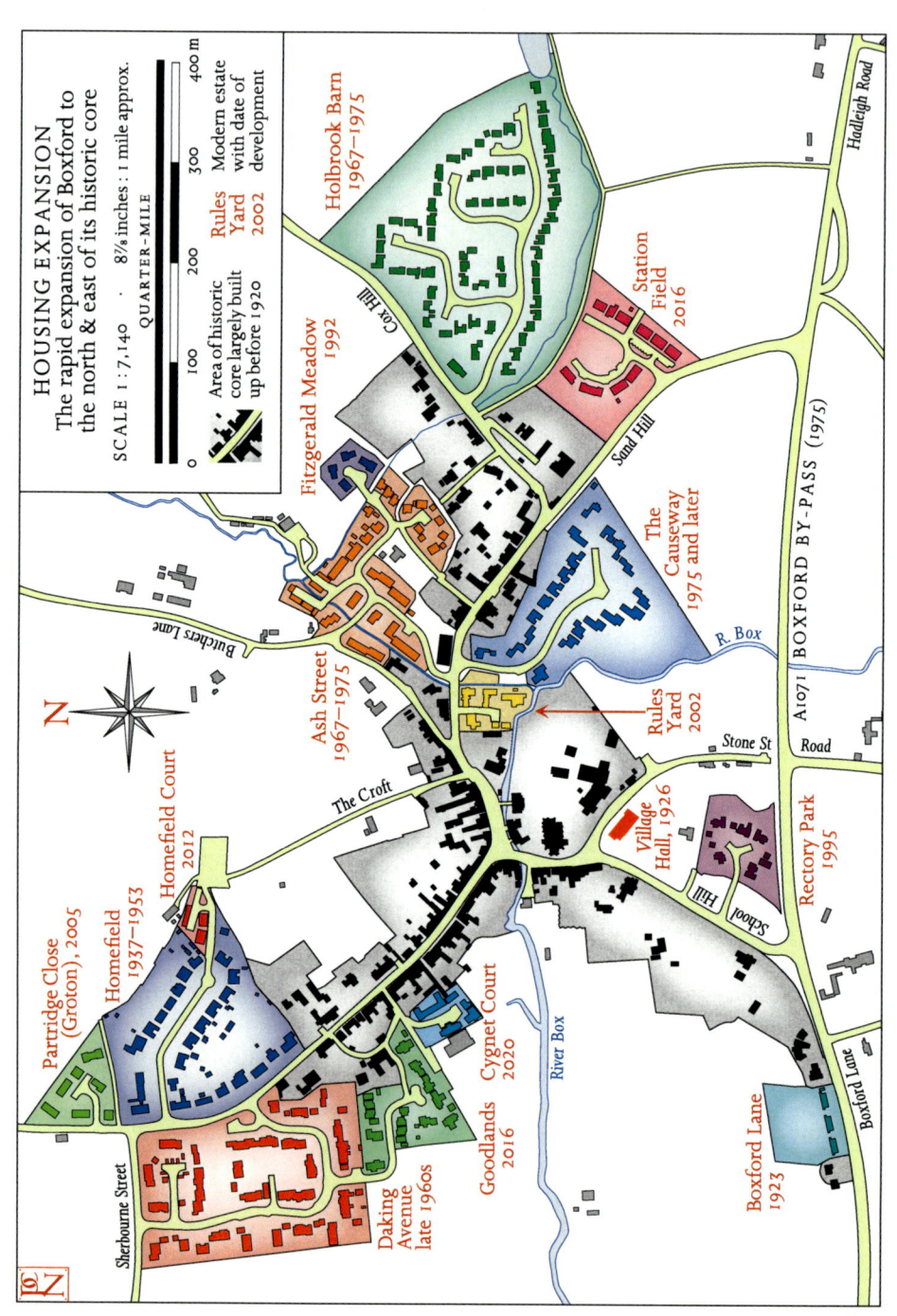

HOUSING EXPANSION
The rapid expansion of Boxford to
the north & east of its historic core

SCALE 1 : 7,140 · 8⅞ inches : 1 mile approx.

QUARTER-MILE

0   100   200   300   400 m

Area of historic
core largely built
up before 1920

Modern estate
with date of
development

Rules
Yard
2002

Holbrook Barn
1967–1975

Cox Hill

Station
Field
2016

Fitzgerald Meadow
1992

Sand Hill

The Causeway
1975 and later

R. Box

Butchers Lane

Ash Street
1967–1975

Rules Yard
2002

Stone St

A1071 BOXFORD BY-PASS (1975)

Road

The Croft

Village
Hall, 1926

Rectory Park
1995

Homefield Court
2012

School Hill

Homefield
1937–1953

Partridge Close
(Groton), 2005

Sherbourne Street

N

Goodlands
2016

Cygnet Court
2020

River Box

Daking
Avenue
late 1960s

Boxford Lane
1923

Boxford Lane

N

village, as the Boxford Society record of disputes show. Its foundation in 1973 by these incomers was one of their contributions. It showed their desire to preserve what was best in Boxford as it expanded, and to save its historic centre from further decay. Some probably were rather 'pushy' and did not always respect local ways. They had ideas for improvements and the money to buy and renovate the old houses, unlike the existing population who could not afford to buy in a rapidly rising market. Nevertheless, these incomers contributed much to the development of the village economically and socially and in time they have integrated.

In the late 1960s the famous stained glass artist Rosemary Rutherford was commissioned to make a new east window for St Mary's church. Sadly she died in 1972 before it was completed and her brother finished it in 1973. Depicting the Transfiguration, it is highly regarded and rains colour and vibrancy from the east end with tremendous light, even on the dullest winter days.

THE RAPID EXPANSION OF HOUSING

The influx of people in well-paid jobs, and rising wages generally, led not only to extensive restoration of the existing housing stock but also to considerable house-building. People were attracted to this pretty, quintessential village and in 1960 it still largely consisted of only its Mediaeval core. Some of the young couples from long-standing village families were much in need of housing, but they saw prices soar when run-down houses were bought and renovated by better-paid and not always welcome outsiders. They could not afford to rent or buy, as is again the case today, when prices are very much higher. They even saw small cottages being bought as second homes. This must have been galling. New estates consisting of houses of various sizes, rents and prices were planned to satisfy demand, and built in a rush of development.

Brook Hall, Holbrook Barn and Marsh Roads, Ash Street and Fen Street, Daking Avenue and Gunary Close all began construction between 1967 and 1970. These were followed by The Causeway in the early 1970s. Some of these were clearly built for the professional, managerial and technical newcomers planning to commute to near-by towns and London. By this time the centre of Boxford desperately needed a relief road to remove the rapidly growing motor traffic and increasingly large trucks. The A1071 by-pass was completed in 1975 and for a short while Boxford was relieved of its congestion.

Fitzgerald Meadow was built around 1992, Rectory Park in 1995 and Rules Yard was built over the old Rule's bus depot in 2002. More recently Partridge Close (2005) in Groton on the boundary with Boxford, Homefield Court (2012) and Station Field (2016) have been added, with some houses intended to help young people to stay in the village at a price or rent they might be able to afford. More expensive and also some more affordable housing was provided at Goodlands in 2016 and expensive housing in Cygnet Court in 2020.

POPULATION GROWTH, 1841–2017

The changes outlined above led to considerable population growth in Boxford. It is difficult to obtain accurate and truly comparable figures for the whole Boxford settlement from the census, because data was collected by parish and the boundaries kept changing. This is particularly a problem for Boxford itself for, as we have seen, significant parts of the built-up area were in four adjoining parishes until 1934. These are the closest comparable estimates available:

Based on the census:	1841	1,121 inhabitants
	1851	898 inhabitants
	1871	743 inhabitants
	1901	612 inhabitants
	1911	505 inhabitants
	1921	479 inhabitants
	1931	633 inhabitants
	1951	731 inhabitants
	1971	904 inhabitants
	1981	1,352 inhabitants
	2001	1,258 inhabitants
	2011	1,221 inhabitants
Government estimate:	2017	1,295 inhabitants

This shows that Boxford's population declined continuously from a peak in 1841, reaching its lowest point, after years of agricultural recession and out-migration, in 1921. Thereafter it recovered slowly until a period of very rapid growth between 1951 and 1981. After that, house-building slowed and so did population growth.

A major feature in recent years is the ageing population and more single-person households. Much of the growth since 2001 is largely in the over-65 age-group. Young people tend to leave the village to find work once their education is finished. Older people are still retiring here in significant numbers. There is a serious shortage of smaller two-bedroomed properties for young couples to buy or rent.

BOXFORD BOWLS CLUB

Boxford Bowls Club was founded in 1919 on part of the land called Lyncroft. The land was given to the village 400 years ago and treated as 'townlands' ever since. The Club has a very successful history and reached rarified heights in the 1960s. In 1961 four members (Hilda Rule, Dorothy Panks, Mary Williams and Mary Riddleston) won the national Women's Fours competition, and all four went on to represent England in 1967.

Hilda Rule, Dorothy Panks, Mary Williams & Mary Riddleston in 1967

THE PLAYING FIELD

The inaugural meeting of the Boxford Community Council took place at Boxford School on 1 March 1966. Its immediate purpose was to find and establish a playing field. Using grants, loans and donations it acquired Croft Meadow for £1600 from the Tollemache & Cobbold Brewery of Ipswich in January 1967. This seems a real bargain today. To celebrate, a bonfire party was suggested for November 5th with hot dogs, and £8 to be spent on fireworks. Over the next thirteen years tennis courts, a children's play area and a timber pavilion were added. In 1993 a severe fire at the pavilion led to its eventual demolition and rebuilding. Today the Croft playing field plays a vital part in the life of the village, with a wide range of community and recreational activities and a popular annual firework display.

In July 1976 the Community Council helped with the organisation and funding of a trip by seventy-six representative villagers to Boxford, Massachusetts at the invitation of the host town. It had invited the whole village of over 1300 people, but this was sadly impractical. The impetus was the historical connection to Boston, Massachusetts through the Winthrops of Groton and the commemoration throughout the U.S.A. on 4 July 1976 of the 200th anniversary of the Declaration of Independence during the American Revolution. The visit was such a resounding success that it was repeated as an exchange trip. A group from there came here to celebrate the Golden Jubilee of Queen Elizabeth II in June 2002 and a group from here went to Massachusetts in September 2003 during their Apple Festival.

THE SPINNEY

The site for the permanent Scout and Guide camp at Boxford Spinney was acquired in 1981. It is an attractive eight-acre site of woodland and meadow, with a scout hut. It is run and maintained by the local Scout and Guide organisation and used by groups from a wide area.

PRIMROSE WOOD

In 1998 over 200 people packed into Boxford village hall to discuss the plan for a community woodland. A small group of villagers had been looking for a suitable site for some time, so when this well-known and much loved piece of land became available, they jumped at it. In 1998 the land was acquired from the farmer, Fred 'Tinker' Leeder, by the Woodland Trust. For over forty years he had encouraged the children of the village to play on his farm and some even admit to going courting there! He is still fondly remembered by many who are now well into their retirement. Primrose Wood was created through the 'Woods on your Doorstep' project to celebrate the millennium in 2000/2001 and was named after Fred's wife. In 2002 Fred passed away and he was buried in a marked grave in the wood at his request.

The initial nine hectares (twenty-two acres) of land was purchased with funds from various charitable sources and over £30,000 was raised in just a few weeks by village families. Here the River Box, lined with alder and willow, ran through attractive, rolling, valley pastureland. The higher ground was planted by the Woodland Trust with help and some extra trees from villagers and children in November 1998. The 5000 trees have become woodland which is now quite mature. The rest is managed as unimproved grassland and wet meadow habitat which is all too rare elsewhere. Part of the water meadow is a County Wildlife Site to protect the southern marsh orchids and other water-loving plants and creatures found there. Further land to the east was acquired by the Woodland Trust as part of a community levy arising from the building of Goodlands in 2016. This brought the total area of Primrose Wood to 11.5 hectares (28.6 acres). In January 2020 this too was planted up using traditional English woodland species, but leaving a fine view of the church from the seat on the hill provided by the community.

THE BOX RIVER NEWS

For many years we have been fortunate to have our very own monthly local newspaper, the *Box River News*. This records and publicises life and activities in the village and adds to its vitality, linking villager to villager across the Box River Benefice, comprising Boxford, Edwardstone, Groton, Little Waldingfield and Newton.

The green heart of Boxford from the bench in the meadow at Primrose Wood, before it was planted with native species in January 2020.

II
THE FUTURE

As I write this in April 2020 the Covid-19 virus is ravaging the world and our people. Boxford, like everywhere else in the U.K., is in 'lockdown' and holding its breath about what the future will bring. Abruptly the succession of aircraft overhead, descending into Luton and Stansted, has stopped. All our travel plans are halted and we look again first to our village for many of our needs, as they did in times past. Within days of the lockdown our Community Hub was up and running with over eighty volunteers and their mobile phones. The village has come together across the generations to deliver food and medicine to those needing to isolate themselves and a comforting phone call to those alone or scared. Our village shops with their shorter supply chains have come to our rescue. We are forbidden to travel except for essential purposes and some of the fresh food and staples we take for granted are no longer available in nearby supermarkets anyway. We should remember this communal solidarity when it is all over.

The present pollution-free, eerie quiet in the village under lockdown is such a contrast to 'normality'. For some years, rising car ownership has increasingly threatened the quality of life and our heritage in the historic core of the village, as well as the health of the planet. Twenty-five years ago it was still possible to take a photograph of Broad Street and Church Street without a car in sight. Today the village centre is often continuously clogged. After this life-changing pandemic, will more estates of forty to sixty houses be approved, adding significantly to the cars in the heart of the village and wreaking further damage on our infrastructure, or will we seek

The historic heart of Boxford from the north-east in 2018. The parish contains 86 Grade II-listed buildings & St Mary's church is Grade I.

new ways of living, embracing a low-carbon future? Boxford is again designated a 'Core Village' in the new Babergh District Council Joint Local Plan which runs to 2037. This means we have to take at least our allocation of new housing, as required by the government. Already developers are circling like vultures over several sites. We shall need an approved Boxford Neighbourhood Plan if we are to protect the village from inappropriate housing development and undue pressure on our unique centre over the coming years

Modern intensive farming methods are certainly not sustainable in the long term. The ever increasing yields brought by fertilisers, pesticides, herbicides and technology have been slowing. The continuous cropping without rotation that these have made possible here and everywhere is damaging the soil structure beyond repair. The output of food from farming is bound to fall in the longer term. Boxford farming is part of a worldwide system that is depleting fossil fuels to achieve current output, whilst adding still more carbon to the atmosphere and causing climate heating, with all its consequences for the planet. Our intensive, high carbon farming methods have destroyed hedgerows and reduced wildlife and plant species to a point where we are concerned that there are no longer enough bees and insects to pollinate our crops. The Earth seems to be 'biting' us back in so many ways. Covid-19 is just the most immediate painful example. Mostly this is because of our seeming inability to inhabit the Earth sensitively and sustainably.

Our world will be permanently changed by this epidemic, but we do not yet know how. In 1349 the Black Death was a major disruptor and we have seen that it led to significant changes in many areas of the economy and society. The fragility of our system, society and way of life has been brutally revealed by today's pandemic and our necessarily drastic response to counter it. We have discovered who really are the 'essential workers' in our society. Not only teachers and workers in the National Health Service and emergency services, but a whole range of other taken-for-granted, low paid people, many in vital public services. These include care workers, shop workers, cleaners, waste collectors, fruit pickers, taxi drivers, bus drivers and many more. Without these people we now know our society would fail to function. Most of these jobs are vital and will not easily be replaced by artificial intelligence, even if we wanted them to be.

Dare we hope that this pandemic is a major turning point that will bring us together collaboratively as a community, country and world to address some of the issues facing our planet? Global organisations have been weakened of late, but the World Health Organisation shows how important they could be. We shall need to abandon nationalism and division to collaborate and deal with the climate emergency of global heating that is upon us. It is already bearing down hard on the related issues of population pressure, migration and the inequitable distribution of wealth, resources and opportunity. Such problems will only be solved by global collaboration. The alternative of ever increasing competition for diminishing resources would have terrible consequences for humanity. I believe we can change the focus of our economy to meet these challenges locally and globally. It will be hard to abandon our blind quest for maximum economic growth, but if we do not, it will be at the expense of the planet and our village.

The major challenge, as always, will be human. Our ability to adapt to deal with major crises has been our great strength in the past and is our hope for the future. We shall need all of our humanity and ingenuity to solve these problems. If we do not address global heating, nature will decide and the impact will be far greater than Covid-19. It must not be 'every man for himself', with the inevitable ongoing strife that will result from the fight for a decreasing share of the Earth's finite resources. I believe that, through close collaboration with our neighbours and allies and those of like mind and purpose, we can put Covid-19 and the disunity of Brexit behind us and succeed. Boxford needs to be ready and willing to make its contribution.

ABOUT THE AUTHOR

ROGER Loose came to live at Ancient House in Ellis Street, Boxford in 1994. The village's unique atmosphere and Mediaeval heritage were the attraction, as well as the historic house. His lifetime interest in local history meant that, from the beginning, he set about finding out all he could about the village, and especially interviewing the 'old Boxfordians'.

After education at March Grammar School in Cambridgeshire and Selwyn College, Cambridge, Roger began a long career in teaching and education management. His degree in geography gave him a love of maps and landscapes which has supported his research well. Before Boxford he lived in four very different but historically rewarding towns—Bury St Edmunds, Alnwick (Northumberland), Lowestoft and Hadleigh—but Boxford is the high point.

Since their arrival here, Roger and his wife Tina have been members and, for fifteen years officers, of the Boxford Society, for which Tina maintains the village archive and Roger its digital side. This has served him very well in the writing of this book, as have his researches for the several historical talks he has given over the years.

FURTHER READING

Other books about the history of Boxford published by Orphean Press:

BOXFORD: A MISCELLANY
by Jenny Robinson
108 pages, including three maps and twenty-one illustrations
Second edition, 2012, published on behalf of the Boxford Society

IN the words of the late Philip Rich, former chairman of the Boxford Society, this book is 'a fascinating study of many disparate facets of old Boxford life'. It is the result of nearly forty years of historical research which, in her words, gave the author 'many hours of absorbing interest and entertainment . . . I feel that the characters I have encountered on the way have all become friends.'

MEMORIALS & MONUMENTS
IN THE PARISH CHURCH OF ST MARY · BOXFORD · SUFFOLK
by Philip Rich
including a chronology of St Mary's Church by Peter Newble
110 pages, including seven plans and thirty illustrations
First edition, 2018, published in aid of St Mary's, Boxford

THE author, a faithful member of the congregation of St Mary's, diligently researched every memorial and monument in this fine 'wool church', revealing glimpses into villagers' lives over many centuries. Augmented by a history of the church and a biographical index of the people mentioned, it was published posthumously in his memory. It is an essential guide for anyone exploring the building or the village.

INDEX

159